Transforming Catholicism

Transforming Catholicism

Liturgical Change in the Vatican II Church

David R. Maines and Michael J. McCallion

LEXINGTON BOOKS

A division of
ROWMAN & LITTLEFIELD PUBLISHERS, INC.
Lanham • Boulder • New York • Toronto • Plymouth, UK

LEXINGTON BOOKS

A division of Rowman & Littlefield Publishers, Inc.
A wholly owned subsidary of The Rowman & Littlefield Publishing Group, Inc.
4501 Forbes Boulevard, Suite 200
Lanham, MD 20706

Estover Road
Plymouth PL6 7PY
United Kingdom

British Library Cataloguing in Publication Information Available

Library of Congress Cataloging-in-Publication Data

Maines, David R.
  Transforming Catholicism : liturgical change in the Vatican II church / David R. Maines
and Michael McCallion.
      p. cm.
  Includes bibliographical references (p.   ) and index.
  ISBN-13: 978-0-7391-1802-3 (cloth : alk. paper)
  ISBN-10: 0-7391-1802-1 (cloth : alk. paper)
  ISBN-13: 978-0-7391-1803-0 (pbk. : alk. paper)
  ISBN-10: 0-7391-1803-X (pbk. : alk. paper)
  1. Vatican Council (2nd : 1962–1965). Constitutio de sacra liturgia. 2. Catholic
Church—Liturgy. I. McCallion, Michael, 1955– II. Title.
  BX8301962.A45 C682 2007
  264'.02009046—dc22   2006034405

Printed in the United States of America

⊖™ The paper used in this publication meets the minimum requirements of American
National Standard for Information Sciences—Permanence of Paper for Printed Library
Materials, ANSI/NISO Z39.48–1992.

Contents

Preface

In June, 2006, as we worked on the final revisions of this book, bishops attending the U. S. Conference of Catholic Bishops voted 173-29 to change some of the wording in prayers and blessings recited at the celebration of Mass. The vote was the culmination of a decade-long process of discussion and argument among the bishops regarding Pope John Paul II's directive to rephrase English translations so they are closer to the original Latin. Considering that those rephrasings are elements of ritual and worship, which themselves serve as behavioral routes to spirituality, it was obvious to everyone that the vote would be met with uneven response, despite the bishops' overwhelming support. Predictably, pre-Vatican II traditionalists were generally pleased with the bishops' vote, while Vatican II adherents were not, and thus it became another instance of a contested situation that some English-speaking Catholics have called the "liturgy wars."

If not engaged in all-out war, the past forty years of the Catholic church certainly has been, in Peter Elliott's milder estimation, "an era when liturgical confusion and innovations linger."[1] That confusion has been encased in larger confusions intrinsic to the purposeful change and its unanticipated consequences mobilized by official church councils, which are invariably "followed by a very difficult and painful process of reception."[2] Some of that difficulty, of course, has had to do with changes in the liturgy, but also with the opposing vested interest groups that every Church council inevitably creates. For example, Vatican II supporters challenged those who had become used to decades of seemingly unlimited authority confirmed by the Council of Trent and Vatican I, while at the same time seeing themselves as more empowered if not ennobled.

While we can justly regard such repositionings as part of the political context of sacred things and how they are acted toward, and are manifestly significant in their own right, we must acknowledge that the theological content of Vatican II was significant as well. Hermann Pottmeyer, who thinks of Vatican II as a "transitional council," underscores its significance in terms of the sheer quantity of text produced.[3] While all Catholic church councils together, he reports, have provided 37,727 lines of text, Vatican II alone produced an astonishing *one-third* of that total (12,179 lines), with nearly *one-half* of that text pertaining to pastoral and social problems. It is little wonder, accordingly, that Vatican II is widely regarded as primarily a pastoral council that focused on worship, justice, and church ministry. It is with some measure of irony, therefore, that Vatican II's pastoral emphasis on a "renewed fidelity to the gospel"[4] may have functioned as the very theological substance for the confusion, difficulties, and pain that various commentators have found in its wake. Indeed, and as we will discuss in some detail, the "renewal" and pastoral challenge rested in a radical (for Catholics, at least) redefinition of the spiritual hierarchy and the locus of agency in worship practices. Luis Maldonado goes to the heart of the matter brought about by this radical redefinition in his assessment of what he calls the "structure of liturgical celebration:"[5]

> Who is the subject (agent) of Christian celebration? The answer of some contemporary liturgists is that the subject of the celebration is the assembly, the entire assembly. The active subject is therefore not the priest (bishop or presbyter) considered in isolation from the rest of the faithful, as was thought before the Council when in discussion of the 'celebrant' mention was made only of the priest or bishop.

This relocation of agency tilts the spiritual hierarchy in dramatic ways. To take a particular instance of this relocation, the priest does not speak *to* the laity, but rather celebrates the gift of God's love *with* the laity. Likewise, the laity does not passively *receive* God's blessings from the priest, but actively *experiences and reflects upon* the meaning of God's presence. In effect, this tilting of agency constituted a radical redefinition of the division of spiritual labor that no one completely understood, let alone imagined how it would be played out in actual diocesan and parish practices.

Clearly, the Catholic church was struggling with its central and iconic value of community. At its base, questions were raised about what community means, what is an assembly, what is the relation of individuals to the full assembly, what is a proper hierarchy, how is piety practiced? These were both rhetorical and organic struggles, but they were infused with background questions that were historically embedded. Part of any struggle of becoming—of change and transformation from something to something else, whether categorically or incrementally—involves a comparison of what one is with what one is not. In this regard, Catholicism is no different than any other group or individual struggling with change. In the past 500 years, however, Catholic struggles have acquired a new vocabulary of identity. That new identity was largely provided by the Council of Trent in official doctrine stating in what respects Catholics were not Protestants. The "we-are-not-Protestants" vocabulary has informed the struggle over the meaning of Vatican II and the struggle of acceptance of the redefinition of liturgical practices and spiritual hierarchy. Richard John Neuhaus is quite clear in articulating the "we-are-not-Protestants" vocabulary and its relation to Vatican II[6]

> There is much loose talk about the 'pre-Vatican II church' and the 'post-Vatican II church,' as though they are really two churches rather than the Holy Catholic Apostolic Roman Church passing and changing through time. The church post-Vatican II, official Rome insists, should be a church renewed, not a new church. A new church is by definition a sect, and Rome is rightly adamant that it is not a sect. Sectarianism is the symptom of 'the Protestant disease' of reinventing Christianity to suit the circumstances. It is situational Christianity. Many Roman Catholics fear that the Protestant disease has made alarming headway in Rome since the Council. The church in the modern world they could perhaps take; it is the modern world in the church that is so troubling to them.

As a loyalist, Neuhaus invokes the ideological framing of Catholicism as the "one true church," inside of which he implies that some kind of heresy might be lurking in the "loose talk" about Vatican II. Although plausible, we think that such talk must surely be seen as part and parcel of the confusions and difficulties in post conciliar periods, as Catholic workers and laity alike struggle with the meanings and possibilities of the reforms. To some, however, such talk is deeply troublesome, just as the tilting of the spiritual hierarchy and its challenges to entrenched authority is to others. Of course, interpreting the reforms and the realignments of voice and credibility are tightly interwoven, for if the hierarchy is tilted too much and the laity become too empowered, then Catholicism might well become more similar to Protestantism. And that could become a problem, more so than the Vatican II implied criticism of the church as pastorally deficient, which so offended the entrenched authorities, and more so than the question of how to implement the reforms themselves and still remain recognizably "Catholic."

This book, *Transforming Catholicism*, is about Vatican II as a problem. We purposefully use the gerund "transforming" to signify our view of Vatican II as an historical fact as opposed to an historical accomplishment. That is, Vatican II not only happened, but is continuing to happen as it finds its way into the dialogues and organizational processes of dioceses, parishes, and other venues of relevance. In some areas, it may well only be lingering, as Peter Elliot would have it, but in others the seeds of all-out war most surely are discernable. We are particularly interested in the Vatican II liturgical reforms and their problems, keeping in mind that many other problems of Catholicism as well as those pertaining to Catholics themselves abound. Indeed, many of the problems facing Catholics are also those facing non-Catholics today, and would still exist whether Vatican II occurred or not. Our focus if not fascination, though, has been with issues internal to the church, and liturgical change has become the most fascinating. Peter Steinfels puts his finger on the source of that fascination when he writes that "the Second Vatican Council upended Catholicism's theological and liturgical certainties."[7] In considering those upended certainties and the transforming potential of the liturgical reforms, there has been much talk, both loose and not-so loose, that has found its way into books and articles, and it is clear that opinions vary widely.[8] Fr. Michael Perko, for example, portrays liturgical change in the United States as challenging yet as a gradual and rather even process of acceptance by clergy and laity alike[9] Others, however, have seen the reforms in dramatically different ways. Thomas Day regards the "deritualization" of the liturgical reforms as an invitation for laity to express their personalities and individual peculiarities, and Sister Kathleen Hughes has concluded that the reforms were an outright failure in which Catholics have "lost touch with the heart of the liturgy."[10] Steinfels himself writes that "nothing else touched ordinary Catholics so immediately and tangibly as the changes in the liturgy."[11] Yet, he critiques all commentary, his included, by observing that "Experts in Catholic worship regularly fill scholarly journals with articles on liturgical history and theory, but there appears to be an almost complete lack of empirical study of what actually is happening in parishes."[12]

It is at that very point that works such as *Transforming Catholicism* become relevant, since this book is exactly an empirical study of the implementation of Vatican II liturgical reforms.[13] We have conducted a series of studies of liturgy and liturgists in the Archdiocese of Detroit during the past decade, and herein report on our findings and thinking regarding these matters. We have theorized the sixteen constitutions produced by Vatican II as policy statements insofar as each identifies a set of problems pertaining to various areas of church life and then proposes lines of action to be taken as solutions to those problems. We agree in one sense with Neuhaus that these solutions did not attempt to create a new church, but instead sought to clarify and reclaim what church leaders felt were strengths that had been lost and to correct errors of the past. This may be the feature that Pottmeyer detected in depicting Vatican II as a "transitional council" insofar as it simultaneously sought to bolster some traditions and to create new paths of conduct and belief. In both cases, the conciliar and postconciliar documents of Vatican II attempted to move Catholicism into a future that was at best translucent, and the general intention of those documents, like all policies, was to improve the situations at hand. Our question therefore is the fundamental one that all policy analysts ask: how are the intentions of policy makers translated into action, and to what extent is the resulting action in accordance with the policy intentions?

The views we express in this book are our own, but some of them have appeared elsewhere in different forms. Chapter 3 on liturgists as a social movement is a revision of a chapter we published in *Research in Social Movements,*

Conflict, and Change (JAI Press, 1999), edited by Michael Dobkowski and Isidor Wallimann; a version of Chapter 4, which we have entitled "Bob the Liturgist," appeared in *Current Research on Occupations and Professions* (JAI Press, 2000), edited by Helena Z. Lopata and Kevin Hensen; and Chapter 5 on first communion is a revision of an article we published in the *Journal of Contemporary Ethnography* (1996). Bits and pieces of other chapters have been presented at various conferences over the years, and our ideas have been worked through with the help of friends and colleagues. Scott Hunt and Jo Reger were particularly helpful with our work on social movements, Peter Hall was kind enough to read an early draft of Chapter 1, Mike Katovich made suggestions on several papers we wrote on the RCIA, Helena Lopata helped us with material in Chapter 4, and Steve Wolfel engaged us in many discussions of first holy communion. Catherine Wagner, Director of the Archdiocese of Detroit Department of Parish Life and Services, gave us access to diocesan and parish-level data as well as supporting our research in the parishes. The Eli Lilly Foundation provided research support to Mike McCallion, out of which the data in Chapter 4 came, and Oakland University awarded David Maines a research fellowship in summer, 2000 as well as a developmental leave in the fall semester, 1999 to attend classes at the Sacred Heart Major Seminary. We extend a special "thank you" to Lucy Zalewa, our secretary, for her patience and her gift for paying attention to detail. Having the book camera-ready for the publisher, Lexington Books, was completely her doing. All in all, the discussion with our colleagues and support of our institutions has helped to keep us going and has contributed to the value of our work. Finally, we extend our appreciation to a community of friends who expressed interest in the book: Melissa at the pool hall, Jane and Doug at the dentist office, Jack and Kathy next door, Abdi and Lul down the street, the guys at the golf course—especially Jim Brock and Dave Pietchota even though Jim said he will wait for the paperback edition before purchasing the book and Dave the DVD edition since he hasn't read 200 pages in 5 years—, Randy at the tobacco shop, Gordon in Arkansas, several family members, our wives (Cathy and Linda), and others we are forgetting right now. We are grateful to all.

Notes

1. Peter Elliott, *The Liturgical Question Box* (San Francisco: Ignatius Press, 1998), 15.

2. Guiseppe Alberigo, "The Christian Situation After Vatican II," in *The Reception of Vatican II*, eds. Guiseppe Alberigo, Jean-Pierre Jossua, and Joseph Komonchak (Washington, D.C.: The Catholic University of America Press, 1987), 5.

3. Hermann Pottmeyer, "A New Phase in the Reception of Vatican II: Twenty Years

of Interpretation of the Council," in *The Reception of Vatrican II*, eds. Guiseppe Alberigo, Jean-Pierre Jossua, and Joseph Komonchak (Washington, D.C.: The Catholic University of America Press, 1987), 28.

4. Guiseppe Alberigo, "The Christian Situation," 17.

5. Luis Maldonado, "Liturgy as Communal Enterprise," in *The Reception of Vatican II*, eds. Guiseppe Alberigo, Jean-Pierre Jossua, and Joseph Komonchak (Washington, D.C.: The Catholic University of America Press, 1987), 314.

6. Richard John Neuhaus, *The Catholic Moment* (New York: Harper and Row, 1987), 3.

7. Peter Steinfels, *A People Adrift: The Crisis of the Roman Catholic Church in America* (New York: Simon and Schuster, 2005), 5.

8. Mark S. Massa, *Catholics and American Culture* (New York: The Crossroad Publishing Co. 1999); Mary Jo Weaver and R. Scott Appleby, eds., *Being Right: Conservative Catholics in America* (Bloomington, IN: Indiana University Press, 1995); Mary Jo Weaver, ed., *What's Left: Liberal Catholics in America*, (Bloomington, IN: Indiana University Press, 1997); Colleen Carroll, *The New Faithful: Why Young Adults are Embracing Christian Orthodoxy*, (Chicago, Loyola University Press, 2002); Charles Morris, *American Catholic: The Saints and Sinners who Built America's Most Powerful Church*, (New York: Times Books Random House 1997); William E. May and Kenneth D. Whitehead, *The Battle for the Catholic Mind*, (South Bend, Indiana: St. Augustine's Press, 2001); Richard A. Schoenherr, *Goodbye Father* (Oxford: Oxford University Press, 2002); Jay P. Dolan, *In Search of an American Catholicism* (Oxford: Oxford University Press, 2002); John T. McGreevy, *Catholicism and American Freedom* (New York: W.W. Norton and Company, 2003); Michele Dillon, *Catholic Identity* (Cambridge: Cambridge University Press, 1999); and David Torevell, *Losing the Sacred: Ritual, Modernity, and Liturgical Reform* (London: T & T Clark International, A Continuum imprint, 2000).

9. Michael Perko, *Catholic and American* (Huntington, IN: Our Sunday Visitor Publishing Division, 1989), 292-4.

10. References to Thomas Day and Kathleen Hughes are taken from Peter Steinfels, *A People Adrift*, 176, 178-79.

11. Peter Steinfels, *A People Adrift*, 167.

12. Peter Steinfels, *A People Adrift*, 183.

13. Stienfels is not entirely correct, for there are other empirical studies on this subject, but admittedly not many. For examples of what Steinfels has in mind, see Kieran Flanagan, *Sociology and Liturgy: Re-Presentations of the Holy* (New York: St. Martin's Press, 1991); William McSweeney, *Roman Catholicism: The Search for Relevance* (New York: St. Martin's Press, 1980), who write about liturgical change but entirely in theoretical terms. However, there are a spate of empirical works in this area. See David Yamane and Sarah MacMillen, *Real Stories of Christian Initiation* (Collegeville, Minnesota: Liturgical Press, 2006); Michael McCallion and David Maines. "Clergy, Laity, and the Liturgy." *Antiphon* 3(1998): 18-21,24; and Michael McCallion and David Maines. "Spiritual Gatekeepers: The RCIA and the Problem of Time." *Symbolic Interaction* 25(2002): 289-302.

Chapter 1
Vatican II as Policy Formation

A widely accepted sociological generalization is that social change rarely occurs smoothly and without disruption. Indeed, it is common if not inevitable that any instance of change will be met with opposition, challenges to its legitimacy and attempts to alter its rate and direction, and will involve debates about the mechanisms of change and local effects. The contested situations and issues intrinsic to social change can be witnessed in public discourse over societal matters such as family values and political integrity, but they clearly are more visible in instances of formal attempts of mandated change. One such area of mandated change is public policy, in which authorities define and attempt to resolve perceived problems by rewriting or altering the rules and principles that are thought to affect the conditions giving rise to those problems. The visibility of mandated change thus becomes manifest because (a) such policy by definition is legitimated change, (b) the steps, mechanisms, and procedures of change are formally articulated, and (c) the intended effects or goals are defined in advance of implementation, as are the populations constituting the targets of such policies.

This book is about the intended changes promulgated by the Second Vatican Council which was held in Rome from 1962 to 1965, and was attended by over three thousand Cardinals, Bishops, and theologians from around the world who met for purposes of repositioning the Catholic church in the modern world. The Council produced sixteen documents, called "constitutions," each of which represented official church policy in a designated area. These documents pertained to a wide variety of issues such as theological truth claims, the place of biblical interpretation in Catholic teaching, the embracement of individual rights and political participation, the role of science in church doctrine, awareness of poverty and oppression in people's lives, embracement of Enlightenment insight, and a reformulation of liturgical practices. Across these documents rested

1

an ethos pertaining to an expanded definition of the place of the Catholic church in society suggesting a redistribution of power and authority. The church was to become less hierarchical and more democratic in its decision making by empowering bishops and local parishes, and the theological center of the church was to shift from the pope, bishops, and priests as the living embodiment of Christ to the laity—the People of God. In the views of many scholars and theologians, Vatican II, as it is called, was the most revolutionary event in the history of the Catholic church.

While we are interested in many of these broad intended changes, our analysis will focus most specifically in the Constitution on the Sacred Liturgy (*Sacrosanctum Concilium*). This Constitution is the Vatican II document that addressed Catholic worship, and it is widely regarded as a radical redefinition of the methods and meanings of worship, especially those pertaining to ritual practices. Among other things, it permitted Mass to be conducted in languages other than Latin, it emphasized biblical sources of sacred meanings, and it emphasized hermeneutical and exceptional interpretations of scripture as the basis for homily. The central principle of this document, however, was that "in the resotration and promotion of the sacred liturgy the full and active participation by all the people is the aim to be considered before all else."[1] This single clause represented a major alteration in liturgical purposes and practices. Worship was now to be active rather than passive, attentiveness and meaningfulness were encouraged through Mass being conducted in local languages, thoughtfulness and reflection were encouraged through scriptural interpretation, and the visual, physical aspects of worship (crosses, statues, beads, altars) were to be de-emphasized. The shift, in short, was from an emphasis on the institutionalized church to the community of parishioners, or the people themselves.

Our Approach

We have conducted a series of studies of the Detroit Archdiocese that have focused on a number of issues, such as urban inequality, congregationalism, vicariate planning, and parish viability. In the course of this research, however, we have had a specific interest in how Vatican II changes in liturgical principles and practices have been implemented in dioceses and parishes, and we have approached this line of work in terms of the ongoing organizational structures, networks, and practices that make up the array of situations typically found in the social organization of the church. Following the general perspectives articulated by pragmatist and interactionist theorists,[2] we propose that organizational arrangements are best regarded as forms of activity that have acquired some measure of routinization, sedimentation, and legitimation and thereby constitute the framework for organizational life. This perspective draws explicitly from Herbert Blumer's theory of society in which he argues that "society is a framework inside of which social action takes place and is not a determinant of that action....[S]uch organization and changes in it are the product of the activity of acting units and not of 'forces' which leave some acting units out of account."[3] Similar to Swidler's theory of culture and action,[4] Blumer argues that societal structures and configurations, including their sedimentations of power and hierarchy, are consequential, but they are not always directly tied to action. Rather, the link between broader societal and cultural arrangements and actual human conduct is always translated in terms of contextual influences and situational demands that confront human beings. He articulated this general proposition in substantive detail in his analysis of industrialization[5] in which he showed that variation in the extent to which industrialization causes social change is a function of the configuration of the elements constituting the situations through which industrial technology is introduced into a society.

This contextualist or situational approach was a matter of considerable debate among sociologists some decades ago, but it is commonly accepted in most scholarly circles today.[6] We find expressions of it in Strauss's theory of "ordering processes,"[7] Giddens' structuration theory,[8] the new institutionalism,[9] Collins' situational theory of stratification,[10] various approaches to meso-level analysis,[11] as well as the rash of proposals for linking "macro" and "micro" phenomena. Indeed, combined with the increased attention given to matters of agency and meaning,[12] it is fair to say that the major tenets of pragmatism and interactionism rest at the core of an incipient disciplinary paradigm in the field of sociology.

We draw three principles from these conceptualizations of social life that are especially relevant for our analysis. First, a proper sociology must maintain a focus on human activity. Second, there is always a measure of indeterminacy present in purposeful action. Third, action must flow through situations that can have consequences for the direction of that action. These principles not only are consistent with much of contemporary sociological thinking, but have given rise to a promising and productive perspective on policy analysis. This perspective is traditionally traced to Estes and Edmonds[13] theory that viewed policy implementation as a "transformation of intentions." A formal policy may well represent the intentions of authorities and reflect their definitions of relevant issues, but those intentions also must be defined and acted upon by an array of subsequent participants in the policy process. When these and other participants seek to implement a policy at hand, they must interpret it in the contexts of formal authority relations, traditional practices, ideological disparities, political agendas, and pressures from a variety of stake-holders that together constitute the contexts of implementation. This view suggests that while policy authorities may well act rationally in the sense of carrying out the duties of their offices, it would be a mistake to theorize the policy process itself as a rational one. Rather, the formal intentions of policies can be transformed throughout the network of implementation contexts, and thus the distinction between formal intentions and actual practices become blurred. In effect, given these processes, policy implementers to varying degrees become *de facto* policy makers.

This processual and contextual model of policy processes has been directly and indirectly used in a number of research sites. Geist and Hardesty,[14] while not explicitly using the theory, nonetheless show how unintended consequences of Medicare payment policies led to congressional changes in those payment policies which then transformed hospital medical practices under cost containment conditions. Ulmer,[15] who does draw from both the Blumer and Estes and Edmonds formulations, shows how Pennsylvania state sentencing guidelines were differentially implemented in court communities of different sizes, local conditions, and court norms for sentencing. The most systematic and concerted attempt to empirically ground and theoretically articulate this approach, however, has been undertaken by Peter Hall.[16] Hall's research has pertained to a longitudinal analysis of how the State of Missouri sought to implement a Federal "career ladder" program to improve education in local school districts. The State policy specified three stages of teacher pay increases that were tied to teacher qualifications and responsibilities, but the implementation of those increases had to be processed through a network of state committees, local school boards, state education board, various agencies of state bureaucracy, and local schools themselves. He shows in concrete detail the linkages among the national, state legislative, state bureaucratic, and local school district levels, and identifies how group/political processes became sites of contested interpretations of the career ladder policy as well as the transformations of intentions for specific school districts. The policy theory he articulates emphasizes that the "policy process occurs temporally through developmental phases and spatially across linked sites of responsibility" and that "the analysis of the total policy process requires attention to action at each site/phase, contextual influences, and the network of site linkages that conveys the conditioning of action."[17] This approach to policy implementation, thoroughly grounded in the pragmatist/interactionist perspective and so well researched and theorized by Hall, was reinforced by Alejandro Portes's Presidential Address to the American Sociological Association in his conclusion that "Because the dialectics of social life are complex and everything depends on the specific context in which it is embedded, it becomes nearly impossible to predict how individuals and groups will behave or what outcomes will extend from deliberate policy."[18]

While these processes are generic, their trajectories and forms naturally vary with policy content.[19] This point is easy enough to see in the variations among government, school, educational, military, and other arenas where policy processes are at play. Furthermore, the relevance of policy analysis is not difficult to see in the realms of religious rituals and worship activities, although perhaps not at first glance. Following the work of Eric Rothenbuhler,[20] therefore, we frame that relevance in terms of our approach to rituals as specific forms of practice.

It is common in ordinary conversation and even in some scholarly analysis to find the term "ritual" used synonymously with "habit" or "routine." While habits and routines possess the quality of repetition that also is found in rituals, however, they are not only not rituals but, as Rothenbuhler contends, "not even ritual-like."[21] To be sure, habits and routines are important elements in the stability and structure of personal and group life by providing a sense of predictability, as Strauss discusses,[22] and thus they are not to be lightly dismissed as insignificant for understanding human social life. They nonetheless differ from rituals insofar as they lack the kind of meanings and affectivity that Emile Durkheim[23] emphasized when he argued that religious beliefs confer significance upon religious practices.

Paraphrasing and adapting Rothenbuhler's analysis[24] for our purposes at hand, we can identify the following elements found in rituals in addition to their properties of routinization and custom. First, they are forms of activity; people do something overtly and typically physically when engaging in rituals. They also are performative in the sense that the activity is normative and oriented toward an audience. Second, those engaging in rituals are aware that they are doing so. People enter into rituals with a preconception of what is expected of them while engaging in the ritual and accept those expectations and the restrictions that come with them. Third, rituals are regarded as serious activity and produce a kind of liminality separating participants from their ordinary lives. Participants may well enjoy rituals and desire to participate in them, but rituals differ from recreational activities in the sense that participants regard them as indispensable and understand that they are not occasions for frivolity. Fourth, rituals are forms of collective activity and contain symbols expressive of social relations and the significance of social bonding. They are typically performed publicly with others and involve various objects that are acted towards in ways that signify socially significant intentions and meanings. Fifth, ritual practices are accepted as legitimate in the sense that the forms of collective activity, meanings assigned to symbols and objects, routines of bodily comportment and utterances, and serious significance are understood to be guided by tradition, custom, or authority.

Drawing from these five points as well as several others, Rothenbuhler concludes that "Ritual is the voluntary performance of appropriately patterned behavior to symbolically effect or participate in the serious life."[25] He contends, and we agree, that this definition is rigorous enough to distinguish ritual from similar forms of conduct but flexible enough to incorporate the variety of rituals found in both secular and religious arenas of society. Importantly, this approach allows for the play of the three principles we mentioned earlier necessary for our analysis. Certainly rituals are forms of activity, they occur in situations containing elements that must be taken into account, and simply because, by definition, they are constraining does not mean that they are always performed in the same way, competently, or without variation.

At issue for us is the relation of ritual and worship practices to social change, which is a broad area of inquiry that has been addressed by a number of scholars. Ann Swidler, for instance, theorizes culture as a series of "strategies for action," and argues that during times of social change rituals assume greater importance for shaping human conduct than during settled times. She writes that "when people are learning new ways of organizing individual and collective action, practicing unfamiliar habits until they become familiar, then doctrine, symbol, and ritual directly shape action."[26] This perspective, also discussed by Wuthnow,[27] seeks to understand the solidifying functions of rituals during social and cultural transitions and how they provide directives and frameworks inside of which people can form their conduct.

Our concerns, however, pertain to questions about mandated change of rituals and worship practices themselves. What happens when authorities redefine the "appropriately patterned behavior" of rituals, as Rothenbuhler expresses it, as formal statements of church policy? Appropriately patterned behavior, we take it, is legitimated behavior in which the relations among shared symbols of significance, coordinated overt action, and serious comportment and demeanor are encased in a consensual framework of propriety. In a fundamental sense, the conveners and participants of the Second Vatican Council, drawing on Catholic tradition and Canon Law, worked through and issued sixteen policy statements of varying degrees of specificity, and the changes represented in these constitutions were proffered as a series of intended transformations of Catholic thought and practice. The Constitution on the Sacred Liturgy was the policy statement that reflected intended changes and continuities in the meanings of sacred objects, the location of sacred objects, significance of sacred objects, and configurations of overt coordinated behavior. We therefore see Vatican II as mobilizing a period of uncertainty and change entailing a breakdown of consensus over various aspects of worship and what it means to be Catholic as well as creating the conditions for a number of unintended consequences. To understand these matters further, we will depict the important features of the transition from Vatican I to Vatican II.

The Historical Context

Throughout its entire history, the Catholic church has been in a dialogue with the secular institutions of the societies in which it has existed. In different historical eras, that dialogue has taken different forms, ranging from embracing some secular practices such as modeling itself after the Roman Imperial bureaucracy to rejecting other secular institutional practices such as the Enlightenment. In the course of that dialogue, the church has formed and transformed its principles and policies regarding its official theological positions, its views on such secular matters as science and political structures, its means of self-governance, and its views of the spiritual community and the spiritual responsibilities of the laity.[28] Importantly, and of particular relevance for our analysis, there have been significant changes in Catholic liturgy, that is, in ritual practices and their legitimation, and so we shall extract from the church's history those elements that have contributed directly to the pre-Vatican II context of liturgical practices. Our treatment of this phase of church history is selective and truncated, but is necessary for understanding the magnitude of the Vatican II reforms and thus the nature of the policy implementation processes that followed those reforms.

The Pre-Vatican II Context

The term "liturgy" comes from the Greek work "leitourgia," meaning public service or the work of the people, and the Catholic church has always had a body of liturgical practices. These ritual practices have represented the church's definition of proper spiritual deference and demeanor when worshipers are in the presence of sacred things. They developed slowly over the centuries, becoming first formalized in the Edict of Milan in 325 A.D. and then further formalized and elaborated during the Carolingian Reform of the ninth century. Liturgical change focused on the sacraments, which were debated and revised by church officials, and by the Council of Trent (1545), they were configured as the seven sacraments (Baptism, Confirmation, Marriage, Penance, Eucharist, Anointing, and Holy Orders). Trent, the marking point of the official Counter Reformation (against the Protestant Reformation), represented the formal differentiation between Catholicism and Protestantism. Not only was the church hierarchy further institutionalized in the Trent deliberations, but policies regulating Catholic worship were decided. Catholics would focus their worship on liturgy—on visible, physical, observable ritual practices; scriptural interpretation—bible-based worship—would be left to the Protestants. These policies glorified the Medieval institutional church and positioned the laity to place church loyalty before secular loyalty.

Because of local variations stemming from the geographic spread of the church through the eighteenth and nineteenth centuries, particularly in America,[29] Vatican I was convened in 1873. The thrust of these deliberations flowed along two lines that further entrenched the institutional church. First, policies were set and reaffirmed that were explicitly anti-modernist and anti-Enlightenment. Church officials sought to insulate Catholics from the influences of Protestantism, urban secularism, and an overemphasis on reason, free thought, and individual will. And, second, the church hierarchy was further sedimented in the Document of Infallibility, which in its intent and consequence, stated that the pope is infallible in matters of faith. This document officially equated church law with God's law, it formally defined the pope and bishops as

the living embodiments of Christ, and it drove a wedge between the church and
the modern (and especially) industrializing world.

With medieval tradition given force in the Council of Trent and the articulated, official reification of those traditions coming out of Vatican I, the Catholic
church in America developed into a set of institutional going concerns that took
a discernable shape. Catholic communities tended to be centered around the
ethnic parish, Catholic voluntary associations, the Catholic school system, and a
set of devotional practices and attitudes tied to the official hierarchy of authority
and various popular/ethnic devotions. Although a social Catholicism which addressed public and political issues had begun developing in the early twentieth
century,[30] the Catholic community was still largely a privatized one that sepa-
rated its religious practices and beliefs from its public and civic practices. This
official privatization, it must be emphasized, was legitimized by a powerful set
of church laws and customs as well as a consensual hierarchy that connected
God to parishioners through the offices of pope, cardinals, bishops, and priests.
Accordingly, the operating church was decisively undemocratic and rigidly hierarchical, and from top to bottom it sought to induce conformity of parishioners
as evidenced in their visible public acts of worship. In this overall configuration,
Casanova writes,[31] American Catholicism had become a "safe cultural haven."

Up until and through the beginning of the twentieth century, liturgy was
simply the forms of ritual practices carried out in parishes under the direction of
priests. These ritual practices were performed within a set of asymmetric relationships in which church leaders spoke and parishioners listened, Mass was
organized into the tripartite structure of the Liturgy of the Eucharist and was
held in Latin, and parishioners had no decision-making powers including the
selection of their parish priests who would perform Mass. The arrangement of
liturgical practices reinforced subservience to the institutional church and the
hierarchy of identity salience in which parishioners were Catholics first, Christians second, and Americans third.[32]

While Catholic ritual had clearly become the heart of Catholic worship,
there were no official liturgists, or specialists in liturgy, *per se*. Liturgy was
merely what priests and parishioners did during Mass. It was a form of religious
worship with institutionalized meanings. In the Council of Milan in 1909, however, a French monk, Father Beauduin, gave the keynote address in which he
identified the rationale for liturgy as an important subject matter that should be
seriously studied in and of itself. That speech is regarded as the beginning of the
liturgical social movement. The argument was that to understand the Catholic
church is to understand its liturgy insofar as the liturgy is the central identity of
the church. It was the beginning of the idea that the church's place in the world
of human affairs can be found in liturgical practices and especially in the principles that have historically given rise to those practices. Out of this line of
thought gradually came the field of liturgy that was comprised of a subject matter (Catholic public ritual) and a set of recognized specialists on that subject

matter (liturgists). Initially, all liturgists were either monks or priests and at that were not conventionally known and regarded as liturgists, but as we will discuss, a body of lay specialists began to emerge. These professional liturgists, who are now part of what Varacalli[33] has called the "new knowledge class," were to become central players in implementing the Vatican II reforms.

Vatican II and Liturgical Change

Two dominant changes with respect to Catholicism occurred from roughly World War II to 1960. First, Catholics in the United States started to become more assimilated, which was a process that has accelerated into almost total assimilation today.[34] Anti-Catholic prejudice and discrimination declined, Catholics experienced upward social and occupational mobility, the Catholic school enclaves started to disappear and Catholic students began attending secular educational institutions in record numbers, urban Catholics joined the exodus to the suburbs, Catholics became indistinguishable from non-Catholics in terms of general American attitudes and values, and in 1960 a Catholic was elected U.S. President. From the standpoint of the laity, therefore, the Vatican I Church was slowly becoming obsolete.

Second, starting in the 1950s, many Catholic intellectuals became profoundly dissatisfied and critical of what they regarded as Catholic complacency and mediocrity. Catholic morality, they felt, had become too unreflective and passive, and the church had become devoid of accountability and relevance for the modern world of human affairs. Thus, two streams of change coalesced into a kind of elective affinity that gave greater voice and audience to the liberal clergy who wanted official change and who were to hold sway during the Second Vatican Council. Casanova[35] captures that elective affinity and its challenge to the church well when he writes:

> Precisely at the time when Catholicism had finally become American and American Catholics had become faithful followers of the American civil religion, transformations in world Catholicism offered broader, more universalistic perspectives which challenged the nationalistic particularities of the American civil religion.

The Second Vatican Council, as previously mentioned, produced sixteen documents representing changes in official church policy dealing with a variety of important issues. The Constitution on Freedom of Religion, for instance, formally recognized for the first time in the church's history the truth claims of other religions. The Catholic church under this provision, although not officially, relinquished its claim as the "One True Church," and church officials and clergy were to enter into open dialogue with clergy of other religions in the cooperative search for sacred teachings and lessons. The Constitution on Divine Revelations placed new emphasis on the scriptures, and encouraged new scholarship and interpretations of the bible. While "divine revelations" were to come from both the bible and tradition, this Constitution provided greater credence to the Liturgy of the Word at Mass. The Constitution on the Church and the Modern World focused on the church's openness to new ideas, the embracement of individual rights, increased political involvement, and awareness of conditions of poverty and oppressions that affected people's lives. These policies led to liberation theology in the 1970s that merged political activism that was legitimated with new scriptural interpretations. The Constitution on the Church sought to equalize the image of the church as the "Mystical Body of Christ" with the church as the "People of God." This expansion of the definition of the church itself involved nothing less than a redistribution of power and authority. Now, not only were the pope, bishops, and priests the living embodiment of Christ but so were the laity, the People of God. The church was to become less hierarchical by limiting the scope of the pope's jurisdiction by empowering bishops' conferences in which bishops have collective autonomy over selected issues, by reducing diocesan authority over local parishes, and by increasing priest and parishioner participation in decision-making over local issues. At the center of this document was the explicit attempt to align the church with contemporary democracies by democratizing itself and embracing the principles of participatory governance and collective determination.

These are but four of the sixteen areas of policy change, but with these alone it is clear that the Second Vatican Council arguably represented the most radical attempt at church reform in its entire history. At a minimum, it was a manifest turning away from some of the policies institutionalized in the Council of Trent and the First Vatican Council, and, moreover, it led to revisions of Canon Law which is the legal-rational basis of church authority. Bianchi and Ruether[36] concisely summarize the broad purposes of these fundamental Vatican II reforms:

> Vatican II enunciated themes from the New Testament and from later theology that undergird the fashioning of a multifaceted democratic church. Collegiality, people of God, pilgrim people, and many other terms from the Council denote an egalitarian and communal church. The Council wanted to draw the laity into joint responsibility with clergy in shaping church ministry, although the Council was timid in providing instruments for such participation. The leading thinkers of Vatican II knew that there was no one determined polity structure in the churches of The New Testament. Rather, it was pastoral service of the gospel, in keeping with the faith of the Apostles that called for diverse joint ministries of leaders and communities, and eventually of clergy and laity.

Within the context of these reformulations of church goals and principles of activity was the question of liturgical change. Indeed, the conveners of Vatican

II regarded this question as the most central one of all, and it was the first issue debated and agreed upon. The Constitution on the Sacred Liturgy was promulgated (voted and accepted) in 1964, one year before the end of Vatican II deliberations. This document represented nothing less than a radical redefinition of the methods and meanings of worship, especially with respect to ritual practices. For example, the document stated that Mass could be conducted in languages other than Latin; it emphasized the Liturgy of the Word, or biblical sources of sacred meanings, as well as the eucharist; it mandated that the homily (sermons) always focus on scriptural interpretations in an attempt to bring new spiritual understandings to the laity; it embraced enculturation—that the liturgy should be flexible and can be modified to fit variations in cultural practices and modes of expression. This document also mandated that liturgy become a major part of seminary curricula. This clause of the document was the organizational culmination of the growing liturgical social movement started in 1909, and as we will show, had direct consequences for how the principles of the Constitution on the Sacred Liturgy were to become implemented.

The linchpin of this document—the principle that organized and gave meaning to the entire document—appears in paragraph fourteen, and is worth repeating from earlier pages of this chapter. It states that "in the reform and promotion of the liturgy, this *full and active participation by all the people is the aim to be considered before all else*"[37] (emphasis added). This aim, or intention, draws from church tradition that had located liturgy at the very heart of Catholicism and was given formal authority in paragraph 10 of the Constitution in the clause stating that the liturgy "is the summit toward which the activity of the church is directed; at the same time it is the font from which all the Church's power flows."

Taken together, these two paragraphs define a point of dialectical tension in the Vatican II reforms. On the one hand, paragraph 10 formalizes into Canon Law Father Beauduin's 1909 declaration that the liturgy is the very essence of the church's existence. Liturgical principles and worship are the over-riding purposes of the church's conduct in human affairs and the paramount meaning of the church is based on liturgical meanings. On the other hand, paragraph 14 completely alters liturgical purposes and practices. Under Vatican II, worship is active rather than passive, priests face the people during Mass rather than the altar, Mass is conducted in the more nuanced, connotative meanings of local languages that parishioners can better understand, and the focus of worship is on the gathering of the laity rather than on the visible, physical deference to iconic symbols (crosses, statues). The crucial shift was in the democratization of the liturgy, in which liturgical practices should reflect peoples' participation in their families, communities, parishes, and the public sphere. And with that shift was the translocation of spirituality—away from the ritual, clerical mediation of parishioners and God and toward the parishioners themselves. Popularly understood under Vatican I, the church hierarchy is where God is found; under Vatican II, the church is the "People of God," which means that God is found in the laity. Accordingly, Vatican II worship was to always and in every way focus on the people rather than on the institutional church as under Vatican I. With this change came a new set of participatory rights and responsibilities of diocesan officials, parish priests, and laity to activate the principle of "full, active participation of the faithful." This, specifically, was the liturgical policy that the Catholic church has attempted to implement in the decades since Vatican II.

Implementing Vatican II in Detroit

Our central concern, to repeat, is to depict the implementation processes that followed the Vatican II reformulations of church thought and practice. Our research has focused on selected areas of liturgy, and thus we cannot address many or even most of the important issues under discussion during the past forty years. Despite these conditions, however, we think our contextual, situational approach promises to contribute to the sociology of organizations and religion as well as to Catholic parishioners and church workers. We have organized our analysis systematically to depict the diocesan context into which Vatican II was introduced into the Detroit Archdiocese, an analysis of some of the important consequences of diocesan change, followed by studies of liturgical workers and how they sought to implement new liturgical principles in various areas of parish life.

Chapter 2 presents a short history of Detroit that establishes the setting for the history of Detroit Catholicism. One aspect of this history is that diversity of faith and practice preceded Vatican II, and thus it cannot be said that Vatican II itself introduced diversity into the Detroit Archdiocese. In short time, however, primarily because John Dearden, Cardinal of the Archdiocese, was a central participant in the Second Vatican Council, Detroit became known as a premier Vatican II diocese. We work through the changes in diocesan organization, creation of new committees and offices, and the growth of diocesan central services as Vatican II principles were put into effect. We depict the ironic growth of bureaucracy and rise of a professional class of church professionals, including professional liturgists, which contributed to divergences between professional diocesan/parish workers and the laity. These changes interacted with increasing suburban growth in the metropolitan area to create significant differences between inner city and suburban parishes, and these differences were reflected in how Vatican II liturgical changes were implemented.

Chapter 3 focuses on liturgical workers as a new knowledge class, and examines their increased influence through the 1970s to the present. We frame our examination in terms of social movement theory, and depict how liturgists articulated their work and liturgical interpretations through the creation and growth of national and local organizations. This social movement perspective also shows the growth of professional liturgists' intolerance regarding fellow Catholics who were not informed about Vatican II liturgical change or were resistant to them. In Chapter 4, we present data from a series of interviews with one liturgist, whom we have named Bob. This chapter shows in some detail the kinds of problematic situations encountered and created as he moves from one parish to another in his attempt to reform local liturgical practices.

The next three chapters report on parish-level studies of three areas of liturgical implementation. Chapter 5 presents ethnographic data pertaining to first holy communion, and the contested situations involving a liturgist and the parish worship commission as they attempted to implement relevant Vatican II principles. Chapter 6 concerns the location of the tabernacle, which in Rothenbuhler's analysis is a "condensed symbol,"[38] that is intrinsic to the eucharist. At issue is whether the tabernacle is located at the center of the sanctuary, off to one side, or completely outside the sanctuary. This may appear a moot point to many Christians, but it has become a major point of contention in the Vatican II era. Chapter 7 presents data on the Rite of Christian Initiation of Adults, which is a status passage involving several elements of ritual for transforming non-Catholics into Catholics. Our focus here is on how RCIA coordinators implement these Vatican II policies, and how that implementation varies between inner city and suburban parishes.

In Chapter 8, our concluding chapter, we bring our data to bear on policy theory, which in turn is used to assess the Detroit Archdiocese during the Vatican II era. We also consider whether the "new evangelization" proclaimed by Pope John Paul II in 1983, and now being implemented in various dioceses across the country, might be seen as filling a space that the liturgists could not fill or whether it represents yet another organizational device in the religious marketplace.

Notes

1. Austin O.P. Flannery, ed. *Vatican II: The Concilliar and post Concilliar Documents* (New York: Costello, 1987), 8.

2. We draw on the standard readings in this area, such as George Herbert Mead, *Mind, Self and Society* (Chicago: University of Chicago Press, 1934); Herbert Blumer, "Society as Symbolic Interaction," in *Human Behavior and Social Processes*, ed. Arnold Rose (Boston: Houghton-Mifflin, 1962), 179-92; Anselm Strauss, *Continual Permutations of Action* (Hawthorne, New York: Aldine de Gruyter, 1993). For an overview, see David Maines, "Pragmatism," in *Encyclopedia of Sociology*, eds. Edgar Borgatta and Rhonda Montgomery (New York: Macmillan, 2000), 2217-24.

3. Blumer, Herbert, "Society as Symbolic Interaction", 189.

4. Ann Swidler, "Culture in Action: Symbols and Strategies," *American Sociological Review* 51 (1986): 273-86.

5. Blumer, Herbert, *Industrialization as an Agent of Social Change* (Hawthorne, New York: Aldine de Gruyter, 1990).

6. This argument is developed in David Maines, *The Faultline of Consciousness: A View of Interactionism in Sociology* (Hawthorne, New York: Aldine de Gruyter, 2001).

7. Strauss, *Continual Permutation.4.*

8. Anthony Giddens, *The Constitution of Society* (Berkeley: University of California Press, 1984).

9. Heather Haverman, "The Future of Organizational Sociology: Forging Ties Among Paradigms," *Contemporary Sociology* 29 (2000): 476-86.

10. Randall Collins, "Situational Stratification: A Micro-Macro Theory of Inequality," *Sociological Theory* 18 (2000): 17-43.

11. For different views on this issue, see David Maines, "In Search of Mesostructure: Studies in the Negotiated Order," *Urban Life* 11 (1982):267-79; Peter Hall, "Interactionism and the Study of Social Organization," *The Sociological Quarterly* 28 (1987): 1-22; "Metapower, Social Organization, and the Shaping of Social Action," *Symbolic Interaction* 20 (1997): 397-418; Peter Hedstrom, Rickard Dandell, and Charlotta Stern, "Mesolevel Networks and the Diffusion of Social Movements," *American Journal of Sociology* 106 (2000): 173-208.

12. For discussions of agency, see William H. Sewell, "A Theory of Structure: Duality, Agency, and Transition," *American Journal of Sociology* 98 (1992): 1-29; Sharon Hays, "Structure and Agency and the Sticky Problem of Order," *Sociological Theory* 12 (1994): 57-72; John Meyer and Ronald Jepperson, "The 'Actors' of Modern Society: The Cultural Construction of Social Agency," *Sociological Theory* 18 (2000): 100-19; on the centrality of meaning, see Andrew Abbott, "Reflections on the Future of Sociology," *Contemporary Sociology* 29 (2000): 286-300 and David Maines, "The Social Construction of Meaning," *Contemporary Sociology* 29 (2000): 577-84.

13. Carroll Estes and Beverly Edmonds, "Symbolic Interaction and Policy Analysis," *Symbolic Interaction* 4 (1981): 74-86.

14. Patricia Geist and Monica Hardesty, *Negotiating the Crisis: DRG's and the Transformation of Hospitals* (Hillsdale, New Jersey: Lawarence Erlbaum, 1992).

15. Jeffery Ulmer, *The Social Worlds of Sentencing* (Albany: SUNY Press, 1997).

16. In addition to Peter Hall, "Interactionism," 1987 and "Metapower," 1997, see "The Consequences of Qualitative Analysis for Sociological Theory: Beyond the Microlevel," *The Sociological Quarterly* 36 (1995): 397-425; Peter Hall and Patrick McGinty, "Policy as the Transformation of Intentions: Producing Program from Statute," *The Sociological Quarterly* 38 (1997): 439-67; Bruce Henson and Peter Hall, "Linking Performance Evaluation and Career Ladder Programs in One School District," *Elementary School Journal* 93 (1993): 323-53.

17. Peter Hall, "Interactionism," 40.

18. Alejandro Portes, "The Hidden Abode: Sociology as Analysis of the Unexpected," *American Sociological Review* 65 (2000): 1-18.

19. Peter Hall and Patrick McGinty, "Policy," 464.

20. Eric Rothenbuhler, *Ritual Communication: From Everyday Conversation to Mediated Ceremony* (Thousand Oaks, CA: Sage, 1998).

21. Eric Rothenbuhler, *Ritual Communication*, 29.

22. Anselm Strauss, *Continual Permutations*, 258.

23. Emile Durkheim, *Elementary Forms of Religious Life* (New York: Free Press, 1912 [1925]).

24. Eric Rothenbuhler, *Ritual Communication,* 7-27.

25. Eric Rothenbuhler, *Ritual Communication*, 27.

26. Ann Swidler, "Culture," 278.

27. Robert Wuthnow, *Meaning and Social Order: Explorations in Cultural Analysis*, (Berkeley: University of California Press, 1987).

28. Jose Casanova, *Public Religions in the Modern World* (Chicago: University of Chicago Press, 1994).

29. L. Tentler, *Seasons of Grace: A History of the Catholic Archdiocese of Detroit* (Detroit: Wayne State University Press, 1990).

30. Casanova, *Public Religions*, 180.

31. Casanova, *Public Religions,* 174.

32. James Davidson and Andrea Williams, "Megatrends in 20th-century American Catholicism," *Social Compass* 44 (1997): 507-27.

33. Varacalli, J., *Toward the Establishment of Liberal Catholicism in America* (Lanham, MD: University Press of America, 1983).

34. James Davidson and Andrea Williams, "Megatrends in 20th-century American Catholicism," *Social Compass* 44 (1997): 507-27.

35. Casanova, *Public Religions,* 178.

36. E. Bianchi and R. R. Ruether, eds. *A Democratic Catholic Church: The Reconstruction of Roman Catholicism* (New York: Crossroads, 1992), 248.

37. Flannery, *Vatican II*, 8.

38. Eric Rothenbuhler, *Ritual Communication*, 16-17.

Chapter 2
Becoming a Vatican II Diocese

This chapter provides a brief history of how and in what respects the Detroit Archdiocese changed from a Vatican I to a Vatican II diocese under the leadership of John Cardinal Dearden (1950-1980), a prominent Cardinal during the proceedings of Vatican II and a strong supporter of its reforms. This change in vision and direction of the diocese did not occur without tension or even outright conflicts. Indeed, the reception of Vatican II throughout the world was filled with tension, conflict, and in some cases complete rejection. Given that turbulence, this chapter describes two of the broader social/ecclesial changes that Vatican II and Cardinal Dearden brought about, namely, the professionalization of ministry and the growing bureaucratization of the diocese. We first provide a brief history of the church in Detroit before and after Vatican II, followed with a somewhat detailed description of the conflictual but growing processes of professionalization and bureaucratization in the Archdiocese of Detroit after Vatican II. This development of Detroit as a Vatican II diocese is important to understand because it is within these broader social and ecclesial conditions that liturgical policies were implemented in parishes throughout the archdiocese.

Short History of the Archdiocese of Detroit

Before Vatican II, a central issue of the Detroit Archdiocese's history, as was the case throughout the country, was the development of a coherent American Catholicism.[1] Given America's predominantly Protestant religious and anti-Catholic culture, in addition to the American Catholic church itself being a loose assemblage of ethnic parishes that exhibited many variations in its worship practices, the bishops desired a more coherent Catholic identity that not only had ties to Rome but, more importantly, to America itself.[2] Even though Rome fought with American bishops over their identifying too closely with the American way of life, most of Detroit's priests and bishops favored Americanization. Gradually, especially after 1890, but admittedly quite unevenly, the church in Detroit became more organizationally and religiously uniform. The main counter-current to this organizational uniformity was the continuing flood of new immigrants through the mid-twentieth century. But as Tentler observes, "By the late 1940s, however, we can speak with confidence of a wholly American Church in the Archdiocese of Detroit. For the process of assimilation was greatly intensi-fied after the First World War, and the last wave of immigrants was American-ized more swiftly than their predecessors had been."[3] This Americanization process created a mainline American Catholic religion that felt at home in the broader American cultural context. This broader, low-tension relationship be-tween the Catholic church and American culture that emerged in the latter years of Vatican I created a more open relational context that legitimized the explora-tion of the church's relationship with secular society as well as internal ecclesial matters such as its own ritual practices.

The Catholic church in Detroit, of course, existed in the broader cultural context of Protestant America and, as mentioned earlier, had to contend with strands of anti-Catholicism that persisted in more subtle ways in mid-century. Politically, though, there was some measure of Catholic acceptance, as evident by the fact that the Catholic, Frank Murphy, won the mayoral seat of Detroit and later the governor's seat of Michigan in the 1930s, even in a historically Protes-tant state like Michigan. Moreover, President Roosevelt's White House "courted Catholics as they had never been courted before."[4] Even though Catholics had arrived politically, largely due to the democrats emerging after 1932 as the na-tion's majority party, there were still ideological battles between Protestants and Catholics. Catholic schools, for example, "had long been a source of contro-versy, and the schools were a principal bone of contention in the years after World War II,"[5] especially over the issue of federal funding. But Catholics were struggling with the broader culture over their opposition to divorce and contra-ception as well. Consequently, a commitment to separate Catholic institutions grew stronger in these middle century years, especially as Catholics became more affluent and more assimilated. Indeed, in the Archdiocese of Detroit the network of educational and social welfare institutions grew impressively after World War II, and many concede that because of these Catholic institutions the intermarriage rate actually was lower than it was in the 1920s. Nevertheless, many Catholics did not want to remain too distinctive, and wished for greater assimilation. Consequently, the Catholicism of the latter years of Vatican I set the conditions for Vatican II's openness to the secular world, as Tentler vividly describes:[6]

Many educated Catholics were delighted by Pope John's call for an 'opening to the world,' and warmly sympathetic to the 'secular' theologies that enjoyed such a vogue in the mid-1960s. The walls of the Catholic ghetto were not impermeable; the most enthusiastic Catholic proponents of the new secularism, indeed, had generally been bred within those walls, which they proceeded to attack in the 1960s in a fine display of native optimism. Only thoroughgoing Americans could have been so impatient with the claims of tradition.

Being impatient with the claims of tradition, according to Tentler, clearly expressed Catholics' thoroughgoing Americanization.

The other big story of the Catholic church in Detroit throughout the first half of the twentieth century was its simultaneous acceptance and rejection of racism.[7] In 1910 there were just under six thousand African Americans in the city (1.2 percent) whereas today over 80 percent of Detroit's population is black. Although many local black elites were tolerated (e.g., Michigan law allowed them to be served at restaurants), the majority of blacks were confined to poverty by segregated labor markets coupled with the vast majority of whites being racist. Indeed, Catholics "were widely believed to be more aggressively anti-black than many of their contemporaries, for it was Catholics with whom blacks typically competed for jobs and housing. Detroit's heavily Irish Corktown district was reputed to be a dangerous place for blacks in the nineteenth century, and gangs of Irish toughs harassed black citizens on occasion in the city's principal Negro district."[8] Moreover, Catholic spokesmen during this time remained largely silent on the issue of race. Bishop Foley, for example, "is not known to have spoken publicly on the matter, nor, evidently, did any of his clergy."[9]

Given that Detroit did not receive many immigrants from either Maryland or Louisiana (cradles of black Catholicism), only about 2 percent of the city's black churchgoers were Catholic, a low percentage not improved by the fact that the church in Detroit made very few efforts to convert blacks. The founding of St. Peter Claver's mission in 1911, however, began the era of the "racial parish" in the Detroit Archdiocese. Four parishes between 1911 and 1943 were established for blacks, with their membership being defined by race instead of residence, as Canon Law prescribed.[10] Consequently, they were not considered territorial parishes but racial parishes, as Tentler notes: "The ethnic parish, moreover, was at least in theory a temporary phenomenon; ethnic parishes were expected eventually to assume territorial status. But there is no indication before the late 1940s that the Chancery saw the racial parish as anything but a permanent part of the city's religious landscape."[11] Nevertheless, most blacks regarded the racial parish as a sign of liberty, for even though racial parishes were built on segregationists premises many blacks wanted parishes of their own where they could hold positions of leadership as well as feel at home.

Sports were one arena in which black Catholics at St. Peter Clavers could reach out to the local community. Being active in the Catholic Youth Organization (CYO) helped this connection as well as the parish boxing team winning the

CYO trophy in 1937 and 1938. Nevertheless, most black Catholics knew they were not welcomed in certain of the city's Catholic churches nor in the vast majority of its parochial schools. Tentler argues that "It was not until 1942, however, that the Catholic Interracial Council of Detroit was established, although with most of the same personnel as the apparently defunct Federation chapter of 1940. The council was the first Catholic organization in Detroit to speak in a sustained and effective way to the problem of race relations in the Church and in the larger society."[12]

After much negotiation and stressful interaction, Father Dukette, one of two black priests in the country at this time, finally received a pastorate in 1927 at St. Benedict the Moor, which was defined as a racial parish. In 1932, Fr. Henry Thiefels came to St. Peter Claver's, and while remaining a racial parish, it started to grow and thrive. The Chancery, therefore, continued to establish racial parishes throughout the period of World War II. Racial tensions nonetheless rose and dissipated throughout these years with most Catholics as well as the Chancery decrying racism and working to curb its influence in the later half of the twentieth century. Although race relations are still an issue in today's Vatican II diocesan context, it is not as overtly problematic as it was in the first half of the twentieth century Vatican I context. Today, for example, the diocese has an Office of Black Catholic Ministry as well as an Office of Hispanic Ministry that attend specifically to ethnic and racial issues. Again, racial and ethnic tensions persist, but in a Vatican II context of greater tolerance. This greater racial tolerance has opened the way for the church in Detroit to examine internal liturgical issues as they relate to various ethnicities rather than relationships between different racial and ethnic groups, *per se*. Race is a factor, for instance, in the implementation of the RCIA, but not explicitly because there are racial tensions between blacks and whites. Rather, black and white parishes implement the policies of the RCIA differently partly because they are differentially related to the liturgical social movement, and partly because of the ecological distribution of racial groups. Thus, under the more external social conditions of Catholics experiencing greater Americanization and recent tolerance of racial and ethnic diversity, the Catholic church in Detroit was in a position to examine more deliberately some of its own internal ecclesial and liturgical issues.

Another important area of Church life as the Detroit Archdiocese changed from a Vatican I to a Vatican II church is its organizational structure. In the Vatican I era, the Catholic population swelled from 386,000 in 1919 to 725,000 in 1929, and much of this growth occurred within the city of Detroit. Already a boom town by 1918, Detroit's population more than doubled in the 1920's, and many of its newest residents were immigrants, with the majority of those immigrants being Catholic. As Tentler explains, "perhaps as many as 40 percent of its inhabitants were at least nominal members of the Church."[13] Moreover, the growth in Catholic population and economic prosperity not only led to a new political assertiveness and the election of a Catholic mayor in 1924, it also contributed to the increasing size and variety of Catholic institutions. By the late 1940s, the Chancery expanded and governed the conduct of parochial schools and Catholic charities as well as bringing several lay-directed Catholic activities under its control. Since 1943, there was an Archdiocesan-wide campaign to raise money for the many activities of the archdiocese, and the success of these drives contributed additional vigor and hope to Catholics in general and Catholic education and Catholic charities in particular. Moreover, a major seminary was opened near Detroit in 1949, which meant that priests could be trained at home in graduate studies. Given this, Tentler notes, "a greater sense of solidarity among the diocesan clergy was quite reasonably anticipated with the opening of the major seminary, and a greater uniformity in their worldview, their values, and their conduct. And this seemed appropriate, for the laity were now a more homogeneous population than ever before."[14]

Although much of this growth and expansion was due to the swelling Catholic population, it also stemmed from the work of Bishops Gallaher (1918-1937) and Mooney (1937-1958) who were both "builders and consolidators . . . responsible for something akin to an administrative revolution, shifting power away from the parish to the Chancery and, in some areas, from lay to clerical hands."[15] As we will see, this is the opposite of what happened after Vatican II. Nevertheless, as Tentler writes:

> What Gallagher and Mooney achieved had been anticipated in the various administrative reforms of their predecessors, for every bishop of Detroit had tried to enhance his own power with respect to his clergy and the laity. But it was only after the First World War that the growing size and wealth of the Catholic population and the easing of ethnic tensions made far-reaching administrative reform a feasible proposition.[16]

In some ways, these leaders had a vision of "ghetto Catholicism" for all Catholics; that is, they wanted Catholics to live in an institutionally complete community of their own, surrounded by catholic parishes, schools, hospitals, universities, social service agencies, and trade and professional organizations. Both also believed that clerical leadership was essential to all forms of Catholic life, and so they worked hard to shape and form their new priests in a particular mold of obedience and discipline. For both, their crowning achievement was the building of a seminary, and though they had similar visions and goals, their personalities were strikingly opposite as well as their style of leadership. Gallagher "was an abrasive and impetuous man, and inclined to conspiratorial, even apocalyptic, views on history and politics."[17] His strength was the breadth of his vision, but he paid little attention to financial detail and when he died in 1937 "his many achievements were overshadowed by the virtual bankruptcy of his Diocese and by the controversy that surrounded the career of Father Charles Coughlin, whose patron Gallagher had been."[18] Mooney, on the other hand, was a meticulous administrator and incapable of fiscal imprudence. He was also a "sophisticated internationalist . . . Sympathetic to industrial unionism and to most New Deal reforms, he had cordial relations with the Roosevelt administration during and after the late 1930s, when he served repeatedly as chairman of the Administrative Board of the National Catholic Welfare Conference."[19] Mooney's integrity also won him the respect of his fellow bishops and when he died in 1958 he was mourned far beyond the borders of Detroit and was judged an exemplary bishop.

Cardinals John Dearden (1959-1980) and Edmond Szoka (1980-1989), during their tenures, increased the bureaucracy of the Detroit Archdiocese as well, but in Dearden's case the situation was one of shifting power more to the laity and away from priests as well as more to the parish and away from the Chancery. Szoka, on the other hand, continued some of the changes brought about by Vatican II, but he began to shift power back to priests and the Chancery and away from the laity and the local parish. Under Dearden, the laity were more engaged in the liturgy, and women participated more in Archdiocesan and in parish life operations than in any previous time. Dearden was guiding the Archdiocese after Vatican II down the path of change toward becoming a complete Vatican II diocese by having more lay people involved with internal parish and diocesan decision making, whereas in the era of Gallagher and Mooney (Vatican I era) the laity served their parish and faith more by being engaged in church affairs external to the inner workings of the diocese or parish such as apostolic ministries of helping the poor, raising good Catholic families, and being honest Catholics in the workplace. The laity's ministry, in other words, was to influence the external world of work and family, not the internal world of the church. Although Szoka was less enthusiastic about such developments, he nonetheless embraced much of what Dearden had changed while simultaneously asserting his authority in a manner reminiscent of the Vatican I Bishop Gallagher. His Vatican I authoritarian style became clearly evident in his handling of the church closings in 1988. Szoka noted, for instance, that parishes appealing their closure would not change his mind. Bridger and Maines detected this authoritarian style in their research on the parish closings: "Priests in particular were angered by these and similar statements and saw the Cardinal's approach as a repudiation of Vatican II and John Dearden's legacy."[20] And although the following poem published soon after the Vatican II deliberations in 1965 somewhat misrepresents Szoka's understanding of Church, it does capture what many thought of his leadership style:

> The layman's emerging, who let him out?
> He's going to cause confusion, without any doubt.
> He's going to start checking, if things are all right
> He may even wonder, if Father's real bright.
> Who taught that chap, to pray out loud?
> He was easier to handle, in a nice quiet crowd.
> Someone grab his missal, swipe his hymnbook too

Nudge him off lectern, back into the pew.
Submerge that layman, lower the boom
We'll have this church again, quiet as a tomb.[21]

Nevertheless, as many have claimed, the diocese during the Dearden years earned a reputation of being unusually progressive. Part of that progressiveness consisted of continuing the internal ecclesial processes of bureaucratization and professionalization that placed a greater emphasis on the laity gaining greater control and power over the inner workings of the church.

Professionalization and Bureaucratization of the Diocese

The processes of professionalization and bureaucratization started with John Cardinal Dearden. As previously mentioned, he was an active participant in the Vatican II proceedings and thus fully embraced the more democratizing directions of Vatican II. Returning to Detroit after the conclusion of Vatican II, he was determined to transform the Detroit Archdiocese into a genuine and fully functioning Vatican II diocese. He worked on this in a variety of ways until his retirement in 1980, and by all accounts it can be said that there was a growing collective effervescence among Detroit Catholics for Dearden and his overall vision, but certainly not without tension or conflict, as we stated earlier.

A good example of Dearden's influence in promoting a process of professionalization in Church ministry (lay people as well as clerics and religious women and men receiving additional training) was his open support of the creation of several liturgical centers that were often located on university grounds and operated as centers of theological and liturgical education. Diocesan professionals relied on these centers for educational updates via newsletters, magazines, and journals as well as for training and ongoing ministerial development of volunteer and paid lay and clerical ministers. The growing number of lay ecclesial professionals via the process of ministerial professionalization, therefore, was legitimized by Vatican II, particularly in the document *Lumen Gentium* which used the more inclusive and collegial title the "People of God" for the worldwide church, and subsequently by bishops like Dearden for their local dioceses over and against the more hierarchical image of the church noted at Vatican II as the "Mystical Body of Christ." Locally and more specifically, lay professionalization was legitimized by Cardinal Dearden in the Detroit Archdiocese when he called for and oversaw Synod 69. Synod 69 affirmed, based on the documents of Vatican II, that lay people should be more involved in the inner workings of their parish and that the parish structure itself should be reorganized to include four commissions (Worship, Education, Christian Service, Administration) and a parish council that were to be populated by lay parishioners. These councils and commissions would become consultative bodies or sounding boards for the pastor on all parish activities. Tentler describes the vision and orientation of Synod 69 as follows:

> Synod 69, as it was called, transformed the administrative structure of the Archdiocese. In sharp reaction to the trend of previous decades, the synod approved a radical decentralization of Chancery authority—declaring, indeed, that the Chancery had been abolished. In its place was a network of vicariates, twenty-five in all, each headed by an 'episcopal vicar' who exercised many of a bishop's functions. In the early stages of this new regime, these vicars were chosen in part by popular election, and their authority was seen as deriving in a principal way from the consent of the people they governed. Those people, in turn, were directed to establish parish councils, whose elected members would play a role in virtually every aspect of parish life. The various parish councils were also involved in setting policy for their particular vicariates, for they sent delegates to serve, along with all the vicariate's priests, on what was known as the vicariate council.[22]

The church in Detroit was moving toward what Bishop Untener (at the time Fr. Untener) called "a process of participatory decision-making," a process that would come into conflict with a more authoritarian reading of Vatican II by Dearden's replacement, Bishop Szoka. Nevertheless, in an interview we conducted with Bishop Gumbleton, he substantiated Tentler's statement that "the chancery had been abolished." Specifically, asking the bishop about that statement, he replied:

> Yeah. It was gone. We didn't have a chancellor or a vice Chancellor. We eliminated all of that structure. We tried to decentralize instead of having everything focus around the chancery which is like the downtown offices. So what we tried to do was to take those offices which had become the Chancery and put the decision making out into the parishes. We tried to emphasize that the church is actually where the people are, where the parishes are.[23]

The theological background for this and other structural changes was in Vatican II's legitimating more lay involvement based on the theology of baptism. One heard over and over during this time that baptism, not holy orders (priesthood ordination), was the foundational sacrament of the Catholic life. All baptized members, accordingly, are to be called upon to serve the church and parish, and Cardinal Dearden invoked this theological emphasis in an attempt to form a more democratic, collegial, and participative church of laity and clerics.

Given this call for more lay involvement, Dearden and others, Bishop Gumbleton in particular, realized that in order for parish councils and commissions to operate effectively that training would be necessary for parish volunteers as well as for pastors and pastoral staffs. In the early 1970s, Archdiocesan Central Services began to expand by hiring more people to oversee the implementation of Synod 69, and specifically to train pastors and parishioners in how to organize, staff, and conduct councils and commissions at the parish level. Consequently, Dearden organized Archdiocesan Central Services along lines similar to how parishes were structured by creating departments of Worship, Religious Education, Christian Service, and Administration at the diocesan level.

Furthermore, Dearden named priests as directors of these departments and then commissioned them to staff their departments with lay and religious professionals. After doing so, diocesan department heads began to train their staffs in various ways. One popular method was to bring in national experts to conduct training workshops in order to assist their staff in how to better serve parishes, particularly how to train parish volunteers in the ministerial areas of worship, religious education, and Christian service. Simultaneously, some department heads sent staff to summer training programs in various universities to obtain Master Degrees in their areas of concern. For example, many diocesan worship staff attended the University of Notre Dame's Summer Program in Liturgy (normally lasting four to five summers) to obtain a Master's Degree in Liturgy. These liturgical experts then would return to their dioceses and train local parish staff and volunteers in the ways of the new liturgy of Vatican II. What many of the lay and religious diocesan professionals worked on in the early stages of the 1970s was how to teach the theology of Vatican II to parish volunteers and staff in order to help them understand how to organize and operate their parish in a post-Vatican II environment.

By the end of the 1970s, the Detroit Archdiocese had gained a national and even international reputation as an avant-garde diocese in liturgical renewal. The Detroit Dioceses' annual Worship Conferences were the largest of their kind for years, and were attended by people from all over the United States, Canada, and Europe. Some similar processes occurred in the areas of religious education and Christian service as well, and by the 1980s the downtown central service agency had grown to almost two hundred employees from approximately twenty five in 1969. The number of paid professional parish ministers had grown as well and was the fastest growing area of ecclesial ministry throughout the 1980s and 1990s.[24] But it was through these liturgical centers that professional liturgists were able to form networks which led to the creation of the Federation of Diocesan Liturgical Commissions (FDLC) in the mid-1970s, a society developed to specifically meet the needs of professional liturgists working in dioceses throughout the United States. By the 1980s these liturgical centers, university liturgy degreed programs, and the FDLC were linked and working toward providing comprehensive liturgical education and training for lay and clerical professional ministers.

During this period, consequently, there was continual structural, bureaucratic differentiation at the diocesan level as more and more diocesan offices were formed to meet the varied needs of the community at large as well as the local church itself. Although the diocese's Central Service departments had been growing since 1969, it should be noted that there was some downsizing in the mid-1990s and again in 2003, but it still employed over two hundred people. A similar process of structural differentiation occurred at the local parish level as well, with many parishes, for example, employing several paid professional lay ministers such as Director of Religious Education (as well as religious education section heads, often two or three section heads for the various school grade levels), Worship Coordinator, Director of Music, Youth Minister, Christian Service Coordinator, Pastoral Minister, and possibly a Deacon. Since the middle 1990s, however, as mentioned above, there has been a decline or downsizing in the number of employees at the Central Service Departments of the Archdiocese and some stabilization in the growth of lay paid professional ministers at the parish level. Consequently, these processes of structural differentiation have created new organizational cultures in the diocese and in the parish. A greater bureaucratic, rational, professional cultural style has emerged where professionals dictate how the liturgy, for example, should be conducted. And this kind of organizational culture has seeped down to the parish level, where, as we will examine, tabernacles are removed from the main body of the church even as parishioners protest such actions. Indeed, some have noted a more bureaucratic than pastoral approach to church ministry at both the diocesan and parish levels.[25]

Clearly professionalization and bureaucratization are not new realities to the organization of Roman Catholicism. But the proliferation of bureaucracies and increasing professionalism within the dioceses, especially of lay ministry, since Vatican II are recent and rather ironic developments, considering Vatican II's emphasis on greater ecclesial democratization. Numerous studies have pointed out that much criticism of Vatican II liturgical change has been directed not only at the reforms, but how those reforms have been legitimated through the professionalization of ministries which in turn have been supported by an equally expansive bureaucracy. Thus, the dual processes of professionalization and bureaucratization have been not only embraced but deeply criticized because these were the mechanisms through which the liturgical changes were legitimized and ultimately implemented.[26] In much of this controversy a kind of battle has been waged between simple lay or ethnic Catholics and professional elites, especially liturgists, about which we provide greater detail in the chapters that follow.

Conclusion

It might be helpful at this point to foreshadow some of what is in the chapters that follow by providing a concrete example of one of the consequences of professionalization that we depict in chapter 5 concerning first holy communion. One consequence of the process of professionalization is that dioceses and parishes have more professionals spending more time thinking and writing about "how" first holy communion should be celebrated. Their reflections on "how" it will be celebrated, of course, is based on the Vatican II principal of active participation, which implicitly rejects the Vatican I style or form of celebrating this event. It is interesting to note, however, that the celebration of first holy communion in the Vatican I period was usually a festive one that most remember fondly and, we might add, one often organized and celebrated without tension or conflict. Tentler writes about one such celebration as follows:

> No parish was so small that it failed to amount a lavish celebration. Festivities typically began at an early Mass, out of deference to the rigors of the long pre-communion fast. 'It was a beautiful sight,' confided young Helena Draw of Marine City to the readers of the children's page of the *Michigan Catholic* in 1898. 'The girls were all dressed in white with wreaths and veils, while the boys wore dark suits with little bouquets on their coats. It was the first time I ever witnessed anything so grand.'[27]

Moreover, even though Vatican II did not develop a specific ritual for first holy communion, church professionals critiqued and reevaluated the integral and central meaning of first holy communion from the perspective of active participation, and concluded that its central meaning had nothing to do with children dressing up or mounting a lavish celebration. This conclusion led local parish professionals to change the ritual of celebrating first holy communion to the chagrin of local parish parishioners. Indeed, their changing of this ritual ironically had the effect of decreasing the "active participation" of some parishioners, as the parishioners themselves note and we describe in chapter 5. This effect illustrates how implementation of the liturgy after Vatican II could be deeply felt by the ordinary Catholic, causing much anguish, tension and conflict.

Unwittingly, many Vatican II church professionals have contributed to the social construction of a cleavage between themselves and the laity in Catholic understanding and behavior. Liturgical professionals tend to claim that they are the experts in interpreting Vatican II intentions, and that if the laity would only listen to what they have to say then those very same laity would become more enlightened and faithful Catholic members. But it is important to remember that it was the Detroit Archdiocese becoming a Vatican II diocese that is the broader ecclesial social context in and through which professionalization, bureaucratization, and various ironic contested situations emerged. Consequently, we will argue throughout this book, and primarily in our concluding chapter, that because of this diocesan shift a number of ironies as well as unanticipated and unintended consequences occurred. Many Vatican II theologians and liturgists assumed that a new church filled with more faithful and active Catholics would flow from the proper implementation of the principles and policies established at Vatican II. Although this may have happened in some quarters of church life, we show that in many situations the implementation of those new principles and policies were filled with tension and conflict.

Notes

1. This chapter draws heavily from Leslie Woodcock Tentler's book *Seasons of Grace: A History of the Catholic Archdiocese of Detroit* (Detroit: Wayne State University Press, 1990). George Pare documented the history up to just before the turn of the century in his volume, *The Catholic Church in Detroit, 1701-1888* (Detroit: Gabriel Richard Press, 1951). It is interesting that his account totally ignored matters of Catholic worship, liturgy, and sacraments. There is only one reference in his index to the term "Mass." Nevertheless, it is regarded as the definitive work up to the period taken on by Tentler.

2. For a somewhat popularized yet well documented account of the development of the Catholic church in the United States, see Michael Perko, *Catholic and American: A Popular History* (Huntington, IN: *Our Sunday Visitor Publishing Division*, 1989).

3. Tentler, *Seasons of Grace*, 3.

4. Tentler, *Seasons of Grace*, 473.

5. Tentler, *Seasons of Grace*, 474.

6. Tentler, *Seasons of Grace*, 475.

7. For more comprehensive discussions of race relations in the history of Detroit, see Joe Darden, Richard Child Hill, June Thomas, and Richard Thomas, *Detroit: Race and Uneven Development* (Philadelphia: Temple University Press, 1987), B. J. Widick, *Detroit: City of Race and Class Violence* (Detroit: Wayne State University Press, 1989), and Thomas Sugrue, *The Origins of the Urban Crisis: Race and Inequality in Postwar Detroit* (Princeton: Princeton University Press, 1996). Paul Clemens' enormously enjoyable memoir, *Made in Detroit: A South of 8 Mile Memoir* (New York: Doubleday, 2005) depicts his experiences as a white, working class Catholic youth growing up in predominately black Detroit, where, as he describes, the majorities were a minority and the minorities were the majority. Issues of race and Catholicism also are addressed in John T. McGreevy, *Parish Boundaries: The Catholic Encounter with Race in the Twentieth-Century Urban North* (Chicago: University of Chicago Press, 1996).

8. Tentler, *Seasons of Grace*, 494.

9. Tentler, *Seasons of Grace*, 494.

10. This was a racist policy of the Archdiocese insofar as Canon Law explicitly allocated parishioners on the basis of residence. This territorial criterion was modified after Vatican II, which influenced parish membership. See David Maines and Michael McCallion, "Evidence of and Speculation on Catholic *de facto* Congregationalism, *Review of Religious Research* 46 (2004): 92-101 for an empirical analysis of this change.

11. Tentler, *Seasons of Grace*, 496.

12. Tentler, *Seasons of Grace*, 501.

13. Tentler, *Seasons of Grace*, 298.

14. Tentler, *Seasons of Grace*, 298-9.

15. Tentler, *Seasons of Grace*, 299.

16. Tentler, *Seasons of Grace*, 299.

17. Tentler, *Seasons of Grace*, 299.

18. The definitive work on Father Coughlin is Donald I. Warren, *Radio Priest: Charles Coughlin, The Father of Hate Radio* (New York: The Free Press, 1996). Those interested in Coughlin's radio sermons should consult Charles Coughlin, *Father Coughlin's Radio Discourses* (The Radio League of the Little Flower, 1932).

19. Tentler, *Seasons of Grace*, 300.

20. Jeffrey Bridger and David Maines, "Narrative Structures and Detroit Church Closings." *Qualitative Sociology* 21 (1998), 333.

21. "The Emerging Layman, *The National Catholic Reporter*, February 10, 1965: 12.

22. Tentler, *Seasons of Grace*, 523.

23. Interview with Bishop Thomas Gumbleton, December 9, 2004.

24. David DeLambo. *Lay Parish Ministers: A Study of Emerging Leadership* (New York: National Pastoral Life Center, 2005).

25. James Coriden. *The Parish in Catholic Tradition: History, Theology, and Canon Law* (New York: Paulist Press, 1997).

26. Dietrich Von Hildebrand, *Trojan Horse in the City of God* (Chicago: Franciscan Herald Press, 1967); James Hitchcock, *The Decline and Fall of Radical Catholicism.* New York: Herder and Herder, 1971); William McSweeney, *Roman Catholicism: The Search for Relevance* (New York: St. Martin's Press, 1980), George Kelly, *The Battle for the American Church* (New York: Doubleday, 1981) and Paul Johnson, *Pope John Paul II and the Catholic Restoration* (Ann Arbor, MI: Servant Publications, 1981) have levied bitter denunciations against the influence of experts, bureaucrats, and professional intellectuals on church decision-making. Traditionalists, who appear a bit extreme in their criticism because of their conspiratorial oriented ideology, have assailed the bureaucratized professionalism of the post-Vatican II church as well. See for example, William Dinges, "Ritual Conflict as Social Conflict: Liturgical Reform in the Roman Catholic Church. *Sociological Analysis* 48 (1987): 138-57.

27. Tentler, *Seasons of Grace*, 167-8.

Chapter 3
Liturgists and Their Social Movements

Andrew Greeley[1] argues that a Durkheimian collective effervescence permeated the Second Vatican Council. It seems to matter little to him whether it was due to the presence of the Holy Spirit or merely the operation of mundane collective behavior insofar as to him there was an observable merging of personal and collective experience. Such mergings properly have been the terrain of the sociology of social movements, and Vatican II has manifestly represented an appealing series of events and processes for study from that point of view. Among those studies stands Bernard Botte's,[2] the Benedictine monk who was part of the early twentieth century efforts leading to Vatican II and who thus provides an insider's view. Drawing from a variety of social movement concepts, Ebaugh[3] has worked out a stage model of the Vatican II reforms, with three stages leading to the Council's deliberations and two depicting the responses to them. Wilde[4] is similarly interested in how the reforms came about, and suggests that theological minorities were simply better organized than the conservative majority and were thus able to mobilize the reforms through collaborative consensus-building.

In this chapter, we draw from the social movement perspectives so well used by others to examine a subset of the Council's activities. In particular, we are interested in the development of professional liturgists, and how, as a new knowledge class, they have managed to create a social space for themselves in church governance and reform. Similar to Ebaugh's and Wilde's work, we focus on intra-institutional social movement linkages, and seek to examine the frame alignment processes first articulated by David Snow and his colleagues[5] that characterize the liturgical movement.

The empirical situation that necessitates the use of frame alignment theory is that liturgists are oppositional insiders, as it were. That is, they occupy legitimated authority positions within the church and fully embrace church theology

31

and Canon Law, but their work entails oppositional change. As Scott Hunt states about liturgists' situation, they "have to argue that there is a problem that needs fixing, without casting the legitimacy of the institution into question. This is doubly tricky for the liturgical movement, because it seeks to alter the thing that perhaps lies at the very center of the Catholic church."[6] In considering this situation, which in certain fundamental ways is similar to instances of marginality,[7] we argue that liturgists do not find it necessary or even possible to bring external resources to bear on their interests, nor do they seek to form alliances with other institutions or organizations. Rather, their resources tend to be authority positions within the church which they use to foster particular textual interpretations of official liturgical documents. Our specific purpose, accordingly, is to show how liturgists pursue rather radical institutional change through frame alignment processes.

Liturgical Renewal and New Social Movement Theory

Social movement research has begun to focus on how social movement organizations (SMO) maintain momentum and grow rather than simply discerning the factors influencing their emergence. It is unusual to find much written by sociologists prior to 1970 on how SMOs maintain their momentum over time. Collective behavior theorists, mass society theorists, and relative deprivation models, for example, were primarily concerned with factors of pre-movement periods and the social conditions that gave rise to the movement. Dissatisfied with this theoretical focus, new theoretical perspectives emerged in the 1970s that produced resource mobilization and political process models. While a positive development, in that these perspectives emphasized broader macroanalysis of the processes that make for stability and change in SMOs, these latter perspectives tended to be overly rationalistic and de-emphasized micromobilization processes, or those processes that give its members meaningfulness and a sustaining ideology as well as the motivation to maintain their commitment to the SMOs work of social change.[8]

We believe that while material and political resources are important, it also is necessary to focus on overarching meaning systems and ideologies, or what Goffman calls a frame. Snow et al., using Goffman's concept and applying it to SMOs, have articulated a series of frame alignment processes that SMOs use in maintaining their identity and momentum. They note that a "frame denotes a schemata of interpretation that enables individuals to locate, perceive, identify and label resources within their life space and world at large,"[9] and then go on to say that a frame alignment process, as they call it, "is a necessary condition for movement participation," emphasizing the importance of cultural and ideological factors.[10]

In examining the liturgical social movement (LSM), we accept the fact that the emergence of the LSM occurred approximately in 1909, but we suggest that it was the Second Vatican Council which provided the legitimating resource or master frame (ideology) for pushing the LSM into full swing. For us, Snow and Benford's argument[11] captures what we want to say about Vatican II's influence on the LSM, which is that social movement clustering occurs in the midst of master frames, which are ideational frames that function as "master algorithms that color and constrain the orientations and activities" of a social movement and other movements that may be associated with it. Vatican II called the church to update itself (*aggiornamento*), in the course of which it articulated a new master frame through which the church claimed its identity. It was this master frame of Vatican II that justifies and legitimates liturgists' claims for liturgical change within the life of the church.

Theologically, the master frame of Vatican II was fundamentally ecclesiological (a theology of church or ecclesia), and was found in the Constitution on the Sacred Liturgy and in the document on the Church. Vatican II articulated a master frame that defined the church more horizontally as the "People of God" rather than hierarchically through the pope to bishops, and then priests to parishioners.[12] This new master frame was placed along side the hierarchical image of the church rather than replacing it,[13] and emphasized the prominent role of the laity not only in the world but within the life of the church itself. Admittedly, this transformation in master frames, depending on one's perspective, still has not penetrated all levels of ecclesial organizational life.

It also should be noted that this master frame which liturgists cling to in grounding their own liturgical principles resonated with the historical milieux of the 1960s. The sixties represented a period of anti-institutionalism, and was a cultural resource quite taken for granted at the time. The liturgical social movement thus was grounded in a broader master frame that resonated with the social and historical conditions of the 1960s and 1970s. Swart[14] claims that an important ingredient in the process of master frame construction and transformation is whether it resonates with larger cultural processes and frames. Dinges notes, however, that in other ways the "liturgical reforms of Vatican II proved badly out of synchronization with social and cultural changes in American society."[15] He points out, as did others, that just as Catholicism recognized the value of the modern world and many of its values, many American youth were finding that world morally and spiritually bankrupt: "The church appeared to 'de-mystify' much of its ritual life at precisely a time when the winds of mysticism and the search for 'sacred experience' blew across an emerging youth-oriented counter-culture."[16] Although the church may have been out of touch with many of its youth, it nonetheless resonated with broader cultural changes of the time and with most of the Catholic membership.

Most importantly, Vatican II's master frame is, in terms of the new social movement literature, a valuable ideological and cultural resource. Fred Kniss,[17] writing about SMOs, clarifies the distinctive character of ideas and symbols as cultural resources, by arguing that they have been under theorized:

> My contention is that cultural resources are different from other kinds of resources in important ways. If we are to use them as important components of explanatory models, then we need to consider the implications of their distinctive character.

In explaining their distinctive character, Kniss discusses cultural resources as varying along two dimensions: abstract-concrete and salience. Along the first, cultural resources may take on a highly ideal, abstract form covering perhaps a broad range of meanings. The more ambiguous the cultural resource is the more likely its level of abstraction will increase. Therefore, writes Kniss, "abstract resources will be more manipulable and thus more easily mobilized strategically in conflict over other kinds of resources."[18]

This conception fits the case of Vatican II's master frame of the People of God and, more to the point, the fundamental principle of active participation which liturgists use to legitimize their work. These master frames, one nested into the other, are highly abstract and consequently manipulable. In the early Vatican II church, these master frames mobilized hundreds of people to take up the banner of liturgical renewal. And even though there was early resistance to these ideas and how they were being applied, many in the general population of Catholics went along—even accepting their newly articulated status as active participants within Sunday Mass specifically and in the church generally.

Repeatedly, for example, we have heard the story of how liturgists would refer to "active participation" in order to explain even to their grandparents the reason behind the changes in the Mass. At the 1994 national liturgy meeting a liturgist said:

> I know this may sound a bit unrealistic but it worked for me—I just tell even my grandparents when they ask about all the changes in the Mass—I just say well the constitution on the sacred liturgy, agreed on by the bishops of the church at Vatican II, paragraph 14 says that the aim to be considered before all else is active participation of the faithful. And then I go into how that principle has changed everything in the Mass. You know, I say that is why the priest is turned around and the Mass is in English and the church is in the round, etc. And you know what, it seems to sooth them if not change their minds.

The precept of active participation was abstract enough to be manipulable and thus more easily mobilized strategically in settling or subduing tensions or conflicts at least for the time being.

Subduing conflicts may well have been what happened, for on the other end of the continuum, Kniss writes about cultural resources that are more concrete, such as church architecture and liturgical forms. Not resonating with a broad range of issues like abstract resources and therefore less useful strategically, Kniss writes, "since they are closer to the 'surface' of social life, they are more likely to be the object of contention—the resources over which people are inclined to fight."[19] When liturgists began applying the principle of active participation to church architecture, such as removing the tabernacle from the center of the church, conflicts and even fights broke out. It was through this concrete level that even ordinary Catholics, enticed by more popular magazines and television programs (e.g., Mother Angelica show), began to wonder and even question the assumptions or liturgists' interpretations of the principles of active participation. Only twenty-five to thirty years later did a more widespread, popular style of resistance begin to emerge. And, as we will see, these counterinfluences were spearheaded by professionals opposing professional liturgists' interpretation of active participation and its application in terms of liturgical policy.

By the late 1980s the liturgical agenda of ongoing liturgical renewal slowly came to be perceived as an identifiable social movement with its own interpretation of the Constitution on the Sacred Liturgy. But by this time liturgists were entrenched in the institutional infrastructure of the church, and therefore any attempt to alter their movement and direction was difficult. But by the mid 1990s, groups and organizations began forming in opposition to the liturgical agenda of constant, ongoing renewal. In light of these counterinfluences it is easy to see how the LSM fits John Lofland's characterization of a social movement as an insurgent reality. According to Lofland, social movements can challenge mainstream conceptions of how society (church) ought to be organized and how people ought to live. As he states:

SMOs are associations of persons making idealistic and moralistic claims about how human personal or group life are to be organized, that, at the time of their claims-making, are marginal to or excluded from mainstream society—the then dominant constructions of what is realistic, reasonable, and moral.[20]

Certainly, the LSM was marginal to mainstream parish life before and right after the inception of Vatican II, but within the next twenty years it had become embedded in the institutional life of the church. It was insurgent at the time of its claims-making, and now, thirty years later, it is becoming insurgent again because there is a splintering of the LSM. The mainline liturgists, who are being analyzed here, are radically pro-renewal, and the new factions (The Society for Catholic Liturgy, for example, formed in 1995) are moderate to conservative.

Because of this splintering, the mainline LSM feels the need to be resurgent in order to continue ongoing liturgical renewal in the post-Vatican II church. The LSM's early reality as insurgent and its resurgence in the late 1990s clearly mark it as a social movement. Understanding the process, however, of how the LSM maintained its momentum and today its attempt to regain momentum is the story to which we now turn by applying Snow et al.'s work on micromobilization tasks, the ingredients of an overall frame alignment process, to the LSM.

Frame Alignment Processes

As noted above, recent studies of social movements have emphasized ideological factors as master frames or general symbolic frames which serve to link a movement organization's activities, goals, and ideology to the broader symbolic atmosphere of the sociohistorical period or with the broader framework of a larger organizational entity to which the new social movement belongs. Frames, therefore, enable individuals to locate and identify themselves within a life space and within the world at large. Ideas have that kind of power of locating and identifying persons and groups as well as mobilizing them to form a social movement.

Although Snow et al. envision frame alignment processes following an orderly progression (frame bridging, frame amplification, frame extension, and frame transformation), they do admit that in some cases "frame transformation is more likely to be predominant in the early stages, followed by amplification and bridging."[21] The liturgical social movement is such a case. Acknowledging that the liturgical social movement could be analyzed in greater historical depth (diachronic analysis), we limit our historical analysis to the period between the advent of Vatican II and the present because this is the period in which real movement and conflict began to surface.

As already mentioned, Vatican II issued forth a new vision for the church (ecclesiology) or what new social movement theorists call a master frame transformation. Given that frames denote schemata of interpretation that enable individuals to locate, perceive, identify and label occurrences within their life space and world at large,[22] frames render experiences meaningful and thus function to guide individual and collective action. Vatican II provided and legitimated the LSM. Specifically, the "People of God" image of the church and the principle of active participation became the master frame that liturgists employed to ground their identity and work. It is this principle that motivates liturgists to gather yearly at the national level (National Conference of the Federation of Diocesan Liturgical Commissions or FDLC) and that inspires them to continue to work toward ongoing liturgical renewal within the Catholic church. The mission statement of the Office of Worship for the Archdiocese of Detroit is representative of most diocesan worship offices nationally: to "continue to work for liturgical renewal through the promotion of the active participation of the faithful."

We argue that Vatican II and the liturgical social movement that followed in its wake is an example of frame transformation occurring early in the process of a social movement. With that point in mind, we turn to the other micromobilization tasks that Snow et al. argue are central ingredients to a social movement's viability.

Frame Bridging and Original Resources

Frame bridging refers to the linkage of two or more ideologically congruent but unconnected frames regarding a particular issue or problem. It is a linking of a social movement organization with "unmobilized sentiment pools or public opinion preference clusters."[23] Sentiment pools share a common grievance but lack the organizational base for rallying the people in these pools to link-up with the SMO.

As the Vatican II image of the People of God rippled through the church, the academic sentiment pools were the first to activate the Vatican II Bishops' call for renewal and updating. In other words, it was through the Catholic universities that Vatican II's message was formalized and institutionalized. A bridge had been built between Vatican II and the Catholic academic world. Although the liturgical social movement began before Vatican II and made its efforts felt during the Council deliberations, it was the effort of Catholic academics at Notre Dame University, Collegeville University, and Catholic Theological University of America that stabilized, formalized, and legitimized the message of Vatican II. A significant result of this frame bridging for the Vatican II church was the production of professional liturgists.

Notre Dame University, for example, created its Master Degree Program in Liturgy in the early 1970s and began producing professional, credentialized liturgists by the mid 1970s. It was during this time that many dioceses throughout the United States began calling for a reorganization of parish life via the implementation of parish councils and commissions which would be populated with parishioners from respective parishes. One of these commissions, developed in Detroit in 1969 and in many other dioceses thereafter, was the worship commission. In order to establish a worship commission at the parish level, however, training was required in the structuring, populating, and functioning of a worship commission. This in turn called for a diocesan bureaucracy to ensure that Vatican II's call for liturgical renewal was carried forward. In response, many dioceses created a worship office or a liturgical commission or some similar grouping that was staffed by professional liturgists to do the training of other professional ministers and volunteer parishioners in liturgical renewal.

Little noticed in this process of dioceses and parishes employing liturgists was the fact that their hiring practices lent credibility to the liturgist's role. Credentialized liturgists were being created by universities and were being hired because of those credentials. Clearly, this professional role of liturgist was becoming more widely accepted and legitimated. By the early 1970s, however, it became clear to many liturgists in diocesan and academic positions that a national group of liturgists was needed in order to pool resources and discover new opportunities and ways to continue the renewal of the liturgy mandated by Vatican II. The perception of this need resulted in the formation of the Federation of Diocesan Liturgical Commissions (FDLC).

Lay and clerical professionals in diocesan worship offices constituted the main unmobilized sentiment pools that the universities drew from to promote the vision of the Second Vatican Council. This was one of the earliest and most influential framing bridges established, for there were now people being paid full time to promote liturgical renewal, and, moreover, they were ideologically motivated. In other words, they were not promoting liturgical renewal just because they were getting paid, but because they believed in what they were doing. Liturgists believed they were the leading edge of a new era in the life of the church, a liturgical social movement that would purify the liturgical accretions of the past 1500 years as well as being enlightened enough to relate more directly to the secular world. Those involved had experienced frame transformation of a liturgical variety early in the emergent phase after Vatican II that embedded and enabled them to locate, perceive, and identify themselves within the ecclesial world at large.

Connecting these sentiment pools of lay professionals and clergy/religious to the liturgical renewal legitimated by Vatican II through Catholic universities was the first micromobilization task that actually led to the formalizing and institutionalizing of the liturgical social movement. The university professors, some of whom were theologians and liturgists who attended Vatican II, produced the probable adherent pool through personal contacts and then bringing those personal contacts and their friends within the infrastructure and master frame of Vatican II's goal of *aggiornamento*—updating the church liturgically and ecclesially. Although there are anecdotal data regarding these contacts,[24] we agree with Snow that more research is needed to unpack the micromobilization tasks of frame bridging. We hypothesize on the basis of Coleman's study[25] of Dutch Catholicism, however, that a kind of Durkheimian collective effervescence was evident at this time; a renewed energy and communal/collective consciousness to start the liturgical social movement. Indeed, it was this group of liturgists who promoted the frame amplification that was necessary for the liturgical renewal to continue.

Frame Amplification

Snow et al. refer to frame amplification as "the clarification and invigoration of an interpretive frame that bears on a particular issue, problem or set of events."[26] Discovering that the meaning of many social events and their direct connection to an individual's immediate life situation are often clouded by ambiguity or uncertainty, social movement organizations have realized that in order to garner support and emotional participation in movement activities it is important to clarify and reinvigorate its interpretive frame. Snow et al. argued that this can be done through amplifying the values and beliefs of the social movement.

Value Amplification

This element comes into play when any SMO identifies, elevates, and amplifies a value of the organization. Liturgists amplify the value of the People of God set down by Vatican II by focusing on the principle of the full, active, conscious participation of the faithful, which as noted earlier, is the fundamental liturgical principle found in the Constitution on the Sacred Liturgy. Paragraph fourteen of the Constitution[27] defines what is meant by active participation, and also defines it as the fundamental principle to be considered in changing the liturgy before all else:

> The church earnestly desires that all the faithful be led to that full, conscious, and active participation in liturgical celebrations called for by the very nature of the liturgy. Such participation by the Christian people as 'a chosen race, a royal priesthood, a holy nation, God's own people' (1Pt 2:9; see 2:4-5) is their right and duty by reason of their baptism. In the reform and promotion of the liturgy, this full and active participation by all the people is the aim to be considered before all else. For it is the primary and indispensable source from which the faithful are to derive the true Christian spirit and therefore pastors must zealously strive in all their pastoral work to achieve such participation by means of the necessary instruction.

Active participation of the faithful is the liturgists' basic value, and it is this framing that justifies liturgists' claim that they are serving the interests of the church. Indeed, liturgists believe they are the main status carriers of the good news of Vatican II which is that all of us, the People of God, are called by our baptism to be the church to the world in that we are to proclaim the "good news," the Gospel of Jesus Christ, to all whom we meet in our everyday lives. Moreover, the main way of maintaining and amplifying that fundamental conception of reality is through the weekly renewal of one's commitment to Christ in the Sunday Liturgy or Mass. But in order to make that renewal and commitment real, parishioners must fully, actively, and consciously participate in the Mass. It is this basic and fundamental value that has ultimately changed how the Mass is actually practiced on Sunday, and it is this value of active participation that liturgists refer to when people ask them why Mass is so different today than during Vatican I days. It also is this value they proudly claim as the basis for a whole host of liturgical changes: the direction the priest faces as well as the people, the use of the vernacular rather than the Latin, the increased role of lay ministers at Mass, and, ideally, the increased role of the congregation.

Belief Amplification

In discussing this concept, Snow et al. state, "whereas values refer to the goals or end-states that movements seek to attain or promote beliefs can be construed as ideational elements that cognitively support or impede action in pursuit of desired values."[28] Values are more abstract whereas beliefs are concrete. With respect to the liturgical social movement, three beliefs become amplified. First, liturgists believe that the value of active participation is serious in that the realization of this principle will lead to a new way of being in the church. Second, liturgists believe that the locus of the problem rests in the laity themselves, specifically in their clinging to a hierarchical image of the church which leads them to an unconscious, half-empty and inactive participation at Mass. Third, liturgists believe that this situation can change through more liturgical education which emphasizes active participation of the faithful in all sacramental celebrations.

The organizational mechanism through which belief and value amplification occurs is through the Federation of Diocesan Liturgical Commissions (FDLC). Professional liturgists, having little success with converting the ordinary faithful, created their own network of credentialized professionals as a means for sustaining their master frame. It is at the annual FDLC national meeting that social solidarity and emotional renewal among liturgists are reproduced and supported, and that value and belief amplification are displayed in an intense way. The FDLC national meeting is the site where the vision or master frame of the liturgical social movement is amplified, reinforced and relegitimized. It is at this site that collective effervescence appears as a social fact.

The main process through which belief amplification occurs at the FDLC level is through talk or narrative. Gary Alan Fine has conceived of a social movement as a "bundle of narratives."[29] It is through talk that social bonds are cemented within SMOs and through which the morality of the group is expressed. Indeed, Fine notes that few researchers have recognized that the morality of a social movement depends primarily on communication. Data supporting Fine's conception of a social movement were gathered between the years 1990 and 1996 in which time the senior author attended six FDLC national meetings. It was at these sites that liturgists' *in situ* conversations and stories were listened to and recorded. Much like other groups, narrative was crucial to constructing shared meaning and group cohesion, and it became clear that it was through their narrative talk (one on one and collectively) in the context of their national annual gathering that the liturgical social movement maintained energy and momentum.

Fine also claims that social movement talk is rarely described in the context of the social movement itself; that is, talk is not situated within the collective action of the social movement. This is what we attempted to do: to collect ethnographic data on the liturgical social movement by listening to liturgists talk in the context of their own national annual gathering. And we discovered that it was the liturgists' talk at these FDLC sites that embedded the interpretive frames of the social movement through belief amplification. As Fine and others argue, "the process of exemplifying a frame occurs through the stories that members share, through the collective bundle of narratives that are treated as relevant to the movement ideology."[30]

A particular form of talk that Fine describes as "horror stories" were unabashedly present at the FDLC meetings, as well as the less frequent "war stories". Horror stories are stories that affront the movement actor and in turn promote active involvement with the movement in that these stories reinforce within the actors themselves that their actions are moral. War stories are more direct and recount experiences that members had with, for example, counter demonstrators, but it is the horror stories at this point that we focus on because these more than any other kind of narrative talk amplified the beliefs of liturgists.

Over and again, liturgists told stories of "bad liturgies" and how these liturgies harmed the essence of the liturgical movement and indeed of the church itself. These horror stories expressed how the value of active participation was not being realized in parishes and consequently reaffirmed the belief that more liturgical education was needed to rectify the sad state of liturgical affairs in the church. The affronts to active participation were expressed in horror stories about clericalism, poor preaching, poor music, poor ritual action, and inactive participation of the faithful (a group unwittingly chastised with great regularity).

For example, the laity was chastised because of their superstitious religious beliefs and entrenched individualism. On one occasion, a member of the FDLC spoke to the entire membership spontaneously saying "that the faithful still have superstitious attitudes, especially when it comes to the tabernacle." Following that statement another remarked, "superstitious attitudes about the use of the marriage candle as well," to which the membership applauded. Many other stories could be enumerated, but the important point is that these stories play on the emotions of the members and integrate them further into their cause of ongoing liturgical renewal. Horror stories reveal the social problems to be confronted and provide the emotional energy for liturgists to go back to their individual dioceses and parishes and continue to promote liturgical change even in the face of resistance.

But in order to change the church and its members, liturgists need to articulate the relationship between beliefs about the object of action and the nature of that action. It is axiomatic in sociology "that the nature of action toward any object is contingent in part on beliefs about that object."[31] Liturgists believe that their object—the People of God and their active participation—is not understood by the laity, and therefore liturgists act toward them as if they are ignorant of the truths of their ontological religious nature as described by Vatican II. The liturgists' belief about the condition of the faithful, of course, is never translated this matter of factly but the message has been transmitted, for there is a growing gap between professional liturgists and pew-dwellers. Most pew-dwellers do not hear let alone understand liturgists' insistence on liturgical education and renewal, and so they have no reason to participate in collective action promoting liturgical change. Social action is contingent upon people understanding the need for change and then believing and anticipating that such change will occur. In other words, conduct or behavior flows from one's social identity within a reference group; that is, from the definition of the situation which is held and which arises out of the interaction of the collectivity. But most pew-dwellers and many church professionals outside mainline liturgical circles do not identify with liturgists' definition of the situation and consequently do not experience the collective effervescent, emotional charge of the movements' beliefs needed to gain their membership and support.

In the wake of their growing frustration with the many who do not understand the "revolutionary" potential of the liturgical renewal, liturgists turn to one another at their national meetings and diocesan liturgical commissions and tell horror stories which revitalizes their moral order and provides the energy for them to go back and face what they regard as the ignorant masses who need liturgical education. Liturgists spend considerable time in the micromobilization activity of amplifying the beliefs of the social movement in order to maintain the stamina to go back and amplify their beliefs to other professionals and the People of God.

Moreover, as is generally known by social scientists, people live in contexts of cultural beliefs about their responsibilities to those groups with which they identify. Liturgists, being no different and realizing that there is considerable variability in the salience of their cultural and ecclesiological and liturgical values and beliefs, even among some of their own, recognize that it is necessary to amplify them so as to increase "the prospect that some potential participants will see their involvement as a moral obligation."[32] Clearly, from our data, liturgists amplify their efforts by encasing them in the language of morality. Indeed, they say it is every Catholic's moral obligation by virtue of their baptism to take up their cause and change the liturgy according to the principle of active participation. It is this principle of active participation, as mentioned above, that is invoked like a ritual incantation by liturgists. It has a tone of urgency in that it is the moral duty of all ministers to bring about liturgical renewal in their parishes. With little success at converting the faithful through belief amplification, liturgists turned to other church professionals hoping to extend to them their enthusiasm and commitment and thereby make them mediators (extenders) between the LSM and the ordinary pew-dwellers—that these other professionals would enact the belief of more liturgical education by teaching their parishioners the profundity of the renewed liturgy.

Frame Extension

As Snow et al. note,

> We have noted how SMOs frequently promote programs or causes in terms of values and beliefs that may not be especially salient or readily apparent to potential constituents and supporters, thus necessitating the amplification of these ideational elements in order to clarify the linkage between personal or group interests and support for the SMO. On other occasions more may be involved in securing and activating participants than overcoming ambiguity and uncertainty or indifference and lethargy. . . .[33]

When such is the case, an SMO may have to extend the boundaries of its primary framework so as to encompass interests or points of view that are incidental to its primary objectives but of considerable salience to potential adherents: "In effect, the movement is attempting to enlarge its adherent pool by portraying its objectives or activities as attending to or being congruent with the values or interests of potential adherents."[34] Given that liturgists have attempted to amplify and extend their frame to encompass the laity with little success, liturgists began to reorient themselves by attempting to extend their frame to various professional ministers within the church. First, extensions were made to other disciplines in the academy: theology, spirituality, canon law, ecclesiology, social justice, systematic theology, history, Christology, and so forth. Liturgy was a new discipline within the academy that claimed that liturgical theology was the primary theology and all other theologies consequently were secondary. Liturgists, for example, would quote the Constitution on the Sacred Liturgy which stated that all seminaries needed to make liturgical studies their major curriculum; a mandate that still has not occurred in seminaries across the United States.[35] Still, to date, only a handful of Catholic universities offer a graduate degree in liturgy in this country. Moreover, in the last several years, many universities and seminaries are beginning to claim that those who have been degreed in liturgy do not have a sufficiently deep theological background against which to situate or balance their liturgical knowledge.

Extending their frame to Directors of Religious Education (DREs) happened next, which was the most tactical move because DREs were and still are the numerically dominant group of professional parish ministers. The role of the DRE was established just after Vatican II, and has enjoyed the most credibility and longest history. DREs coordinate all religious education activities in the parish, usually from pre-school through adult education. Specifically, they help plan the program of instruction for children in religious education classes whether in a Catholic school or not. Given that they deal with children, they have considerable influence and power, but they also undergo extensive scrutinization by parish staff and parishioners as well.

Other professional ministries targeted for extension were youth ministers, christian service coordinators, pastoral ministers, musicians not trained in liturgy, RCIA coordinators, those untrained in liturgy playing the role of liturgist in the parish and permanent deacons (and where possible, priests). But to DREs, liturgists would boldly claim that all liturgy was catechetical (that is, an educational or teaching moment), although its primary function was not didactic, and that religious education should not be age-graded but liturgically centered. Liturgical catechesis (or liturgical education) was more important than religious education; that is, it is more important than understanding the catechism or doctrinal teachings of the church. The liturgy was the "source and summit" of the Catholic church, and all educational efforts should flow from and toward the liturgy.

At the practical and operational level, frame extension occurred at the diocesan level, with the worship office of the diocese offering workshops, courses, lectures, printed materials, and conferences on various liturgical topics. In Detroit, for example, a two-day conference attended by local DREs was held in 1992 on the relationship between liturgy and religious education. Two keynote speakers, one a liturgist and one a DRE with strong liturgical leanings, articulated this relationship. The fundamental point made by these speakers, and what most of the attending DREs took back to their parishes, was that religious education was the servant of the liturgy rather than a discipline in its own right.

Liturgists, then, have alienated not only the ordinary pew-dweller but many other professional ministers. That is not to say that all other professional ministers are alienated from liturgists. Many have acknowledged the fundamental role liturgy plays in the life of the church and have worked with liturgists and have gained from the relationship. But for the most part, most professional ministers are alienated, even bishops, and the few bishops that do have liturgical backgrounds are a minority among their fellow bishops and not all that well liked.

An unintended consequence of the LSM's process of frame extension thus has been a range of fights and other contested situations which need to be dealt with simultaneously. Especially problematic is liturgists' inability to resonate their frame with the frames of other professional ministers and most importantly with ordinary pew-dwellers. On the horizontal axis there is the problem of frame resonance or the low degree of fit between the liturgists' master frame and the everyday life situation of the laity. Consequently, liturgists' insistence on implementing liturgical policies at all levels of parish and church life are often viewed as "terroristic" by other church professionals.

Conclusion

In the long history of the Catholic church, liturgy has moved from being only a set of ritual practices to being, in addition to those practices, a content area about which professional workers claim exclusive knowledge. We have briefly described the historical events and processes involved in the formation and change of liturgical practices, but it has been only in this century that we have seen the beginnings and development of the liturgical specialist. The initial stirrings of this transformational process came from influential insiders who sought to move liturgy from merely one aspect of Catholicism to its center. This elevation of liturgy as a primary concern of church officials was one of the preconditions for the emergence of liturgical specialists. However, it took the Vatican II reform of Catholic worship and the official mandate to develop an educational system of liturgical training to form the basis of legitimation for the liturgical social movement.

It is clear that prior to and after the Vatican II deliberations that a significant sentiment pool existed that gave ideological force to the early liturgical movement. These sentiments in addition to the broad and profound reforms of the church contributed to the social movement elements of liturgical change and therefore made it something more than the mere professionalization of existing church occupations. The church now had a new calling that required new voices to move the laity to a new spiritual center. This was a vast undertaking, and the newly trained liturgists took that undertaking most seriously.

The sociologically fascinating aspect of this process is in what we have called the "liturgical situation." On the one hand, liturgists possess a very high degree of commitment to the Catholic church and the revised Canon Law that came from the Vatican II reforms. On the other, liturgists are agents of change, and in the process of attempting to implement church reform they routinely encounter opposition. And, perhaps predictably, the harder they push for change, the more opposition they incur. This opposition contributes to an array of contested situations throughout the institutional structure of the church, which positions liturgists, as it were, as lightening rods. They are true believers, as Eric Hoffer would have called them, and they encounter the standard problems of true believers.

This liturgical situation—liturgists as oppositional insiders—leads naturally to the use of frame alignment processes as political, ideological, and organizational mechanisms of church reform implementation. These mechanisms are action systems based on a collective identity through which liturgists regard themselves as the primary hope for the future of Catholicism. By virtue of their self-proclaimed superior understanding of the Vatican II texts and purposes, liturgists see themselves as having the clarity of vision to define proper worship practices. This vision is supported through the liturgical solidarity gained at meetings such as the FDLC, and that solidarity contributes to the collective energy needed to form bridging relationships with other church workers and groups. The twin processes of frame alignment and amplification as well as liturgical bridging with groups, commissions, workshops, and educational forums are the basic resources that are used and mobilized in the liturgical social movement. Since Vatican II, it is evident that these processes pull liturgists in two opposite ways. They are pulled inward, toward themselves as a reference group, and in the process they simultaneously cohere into a form of liturgical solidarity and splinter into liberal and conservative interpretations of the liturgical agenda. But they also are necessarily pulled outward, toward the laity and the liturgically uninformed whom they are called upon to transform. These processes contribute to the professional-laity gap that appears to characterize all Christian denominations, and that gap marks the relative points of success and failure of the liturgical social movement in the Vatican II Catholic church.

Notes

1. Andrew Greeley, *The Catholic Revolution* (Berkeley: University of California Press, 2004), chapter 5.

2. Bernard Botte, *From Silence to Participation: An Insider's View of Liturgical Renewal* (Washington, D.C.: The Pastoral Press, 1988).

3. Helen Rose Ebaugh, "Vatican II and the Revitalization Movement," in *Religion and Social Order: Vatican II and U. S. Catholicism,* ed. Helen Rose Ebaugh (Greenwich, CT: JAI Press 1991), 3-19.

4. Melissa J. Wilde, "How Culture Mattered at Vatican II: Collegiality Trumps Authority in the Council's Social Movement Organizations," *American Sociological Review 69* (2004), 576-602.

5. David Snow, A. Rochford, E. Burke, Steven Worden, and Robert Benford, "Frame Alignment Processes, "Micromobilization, and Movement Participation," *American Sociological Review*: 51 (1986): 464-81.

6. Scott Hunt, personal correspondence.

7. The classic work on marginality is Robert Park, "Human Migration and the Marginal Man," *American Journal of Sociology* 33 (1928): 881-93.

8. Steven Beuchler, "Beyond Resource Mobilization? Emerging Trends in Social Movement Theory" *The Sociological Quarterly* 34 (1993): 217-35.

9. Snow, *et. al.*, "Frame Alignment," 464.

10. Snow, *et. al.*, "Frame Alignment," 467.

11. David Snow and Robert Benford, "Ideology, Frame Resonance, and Participant Mobilization," *International Social Movement Research* 1 (1988): 197-217.

12. Annibale Bugnini, *The Reform of the Liturgy: 1948-1974* (Collegeville: The Liturgical Press, 1990).

13. Avery Dulles, *The Reshaping of Catholicism: Current Challenges in the Theology of Church* (San Francisco: Harper and Row, 1988).

14. William J. Swart, "The League of Nations and the Irish Question: Master Frames, Cycles of Protest, and Master Frame Alignment," *The Sociological Quarterly* 36 (1995): 465-81.

15. William Dinges, "Ritual Conflict as Social Conflict: Liturgical Reform in the Roman Catholic Church," *Sociological Analysis* 48 (1987): 138-57.

16. Dinges, "Ritual Conflict as Social Conflict," 141.

17. Fred Kniss, "Ideas and Symbols as Resources in Intrareligious Conflict: The Case of American Mennonites," *Sociology of Religion* 57 (1996): 7-23.

18. Kniss, "Ideas and Symbols," 9.

19. Kniss, "Ideas and Symbols," 9.

20. John Lofland, *Social Movement Organizations: Guide to Research on Insurgent Realities* (New York: Aldine de Gruyter, 1996).

21. Snow, *et al.*, "Frame Alignment," 477.

22. Erving Goffman, *Frame Analysis* (New York: Harper and Row, 1974).

23. Snow, *et al.*, "Frame Alignment," 467.

24. Botte, *From Silence to Participation*; Ernest Koenker, *The Liturgical Renaissance in the Roman Catholic Church* (St. Louis: Conccordia Publishing House, 1966); Lancelot Shepherd, trans., *The Liturgical Movement* (New York: Hawthorn Books, 1964).

25. John Coleman, *The Evolution of Dutch Catholicism, 1958-1974* (Berkeley: University of California Press, 1978).

26. Snow, *et al.*, "Frame Alignment," 469.

27. Austin O.P. Flannery, ed., *Vatican II: The Concilliar and post Concilliar Documents* (New York: Costello Publishing, 1987).

28. Snow, *et al.*, "Frame Alignment," 469-70.

29. Gary Alan Fine, "Public Narration and Group Culture: Discerning Discourse in Social Movements," in *Social Movements and Culture*, eds. Hank Johnston and Bert Klandermans (Minneapolis: University of Minnesota Press, 1995), 128.

30. Fine, "Public Narration," 134; see also, David Maines, "Narrative's Moment and Sociology's Phenomena: Toward a Narrative Sociology," *The Sociological Quarterly* 34 (1993): 17-38; David Maines and Jeffrey Bridger, "Narrative, Community, and Land Use Decisions," *The Social Science Journal* 29 (1992): 283-92.

31. Snow, *et al.*, "Frame Alignment," 470.

32. Snow, *et al.,* "Frame Alignment," 471.

33. Snow, *et al.,* "Frame Alignment," 472.

34. Snow, *et al.,* "Frame Alignment," 472.

35. Fredrick R. McManus, "Vision: Voices from the Past," in *National Meeting Addresses: 1990-1995,* ed. Michael Spillane (Washington, D.C. Federation of Diocesan Liturgical Commissions), 1996: 308-32.

Chapter 4
Bob the Liturgist

Vatican II not only redefined Catholic worship, as we have emphasized, but it elevated liturgy to a place of supreme importance in the modern Catholic church. In recognition of these dramatic and consequential changes in official church policy, the Constitution on the Sacred Liturgy mandated that liturgy become a major part of seminary curricula, and it mandated the creation of formal credentializing mechanisms in liturgical training. This process was not difficult to implement, since it was in the seminaries and Catholic universities that the Vatican II call for renewal was most forcefully expressed. Notre Dame University, for example, created its Master Degree Program in Liturgy in the early 1970s, and began producing professional, credentialized liturgists by the mid 1970s. It was during this time that many dioceses throughout the United States began calling for a reorganization of parish life through the implementation of parish councils and commissions which would be populated with parishioners from respective parishes. One of these commissions, developed in Detroit in 1969 and in many other dioceses thereafter, was the worship commission. In order to establish a worship commission at the parish level, however, training was required in the structuring, populating, and functioning of a worship commission. This in turn called for a diocesan bureaucracy to ensure that Vatican II's call for liturgical renewal was carried forward. In response, many dioceses created a worship office or a liturgical commission or some similar grouping that was staffed by professional liturgists to train other professional ministers and volunteer parishioners in liturgical renewal.

As discussed in the previous chapter, dioceses and parishes employing liturgists lent credibility to the liturgist's role and were increasingly found as Directors of Liturgy, organists, Directors of Worship Offices, pastors, Directors of Religious Education, and so forth. They are directly involved in a range of official activities, including training and formation of eucharistic ministers of communion, training ministers who take communion (host/wafer) to the sick in their homes, lectors (readers of scripture), altar servers, ushers (welcomers), catechists/teachers for the liturgy of the word for children, sacristans to help with weddings, and prayer leaders to assist during funerals. The liturgist is also responsible for choreographing the various liturgies during the liturgical year, especially those during the seasons of advent/Christmas and lent/Easter. The liturgist would sit on the worship commission as a resource person as well as work closely with the parish musician/organist. Finally, the area of church art and architecture would be overseen by the liturgist. This would entail choosing what church artifacts and art are liturgically appropriate and then determining where these items would be located in the church, for example, how the altar, ambo, and tabernacle should be designed and where they should be located.

In most of these areas of work, we have found that liturgists tend to be well-intentioned troublemakers. One reason for this is that they are "oppositional insiders," as we discussed in the previous chapter. That is, they occupy legitimate authority positions within the church and fully embrace church theology and Canon Law, but their work entails oppositional change. A built-in tension thus exists in their work. Their goal, broadly speaking, is to change Catholic worship in accordance with Vatican II precepts, but to produce that change they use the legitimated resources internal to the church. The second reason is that in seeking to implement Vatican II liturgical practices, they invariably encounter resistance from those committed to traditional Catholic customs and procedures as well as from Vatican II adherents who might have different interpretations of proper worship practices.

While these first two reasons are structural in nature, a third reason why liturgists find themselves in troublesome liturgical situations is that they tend to be true believers and to see their calling in social movement terms. They tend to hold rather strict and unyielding interpretations of proper worship, and therefore they introduce situations of irony into the process by dictatorially insisting upon democratic processes and "full and active participation." Andrew Greeley[1] finds most liturgists to be "elitist apriorists" and constitute "an arrogant and authoritarian sect." "They have the truth," he writes, "learned in workshops, study days, national conferences, and graduate school programs.... [and] it is their role to impose this truth on the laity."[2] Our findings, discussed in this chapter and those that follow, lead us to generally concur with Greeley's depiction insofar as whenever there is high liturgical presence in a parish, participants, including liturgists, will report that parish discussions and decision-making processes tend to entail major problems.

In this chapter, we examine liturgists and the problems they mobilize from the point of view of a single liturgical worker. In doing so, we draw from a long tradition in sociology that focuses on human biographies[3] to present an edited but nearly complete interview conducted by the senior author over several weeks with one liturgist as he moves from parish to parish, and in each instance seeks to implement his interpretation of Vatican II worship principles. We also utilize Glaser and Strauss's[4] concept of "trajectory" to give this interview some conceptual import. Trajectories, Glaser and Strauss argue, are paths through organizations, and by focusing on them we can better understand organizational structures and how they come into play in different situations that exist at various points along the trajectory. In this case, we present segments of the liturgical career of a man we call Bob, and depict how he moved through a variety of positions in several parishes, each time bringing to the position his "knowledge class" perspective and how that perspective interacted with the non-liturgical or quasi-liturgical perspectives of others with whom he had to work. We can understand more concretely the liturgist's perspective as we read the following interview, but hopefully the reader will also glean from it a sense of the rigidity of his perspective.

It is important to realize that Bob is rather new to the communities he joins. This point is important because not only does he cause trouble and pain with his liturgical knowledge, telling others how things are done incorrectly at each parish, but that he does so as a newcomer. We believe his "new membership status" accentuates his role as troublemaker. Bob has had training as a liturgist through the Archdiocesan liturgy workshops before beginning his involvement at St. Olaf's, which is where the interview text begins, and thus, his initiation into the new liturgical knowledge class had begun long before joining St. Olaf's parish. We begin with Bob describing how he became involved in liturgical work.

The Interview

Bob: I moved to here in 1973 and I went around to every parish in the area and St. Olaf's had a bishop visiting that Sunday and the Mass was really something, the music was tremendous. The other parishes stunk and the people were not that friendly and the music was bad and so we decided on St. Olaf's and not only that but the pastor and bishop got along well. In fact I got to know him on a first name basis.... Anyway, I became head of the school board there and head of the athletic committee and I was vice chair of the worship commission and I was a lector and eucharistic minister as well.

Mike: How did you end up taking classes at the seminary?

Bob: What got me started at the seminary was people saying to me that I ought to be a deacon. And I kept hearing this from people more and more and so I finally asked my pastor and he said yea I think you ought to go down to the seminary and talk to them and see what they say. And so I saw a woman who was the head of pastoral ministry at the seminary and that is when I started taking classes in theology and liturgy in the Fall of 1983. And so I really began because of the response from the community. So it really was not for me but for the community and they kept telling me this again and again and I believe God talks through other people—not just during a quiet night or during the still of the night. But I have some constraints to deal with.

Mike: Could you tell me what those constraints are?

Bob: Well, when I was at St. Olaf's and whenever I would lector there the organist would encourage me to sing the General Intercessions and so I did. Then one day there was a visiting musician. I approached the lectern or stand and I started to intone the General Intercessions and then the pastor who was presiding just stood up and started signaling the musician to stop but he doesn't stop he just keeps playing and so after Mass Fr. came over to me and he said to me "I am the celebrant here not you. This is my Mass not yours" and then he said to the organist do you know who signs your checks?

. . . . So at the next worship commission meeting the chair told me that the pastor was going to make an issue out of this but that it was not on the agenda. So I talked to my wife about it and asked her what I should do. She said, well ask him to stop and not say what he is going to say and if he does not then leave. And so that is what I did and so I got up and walked out and I resigned from the worship commission. . . . And in the meantime my wife was working on trying to reconcile the situation but neither of the   priests at the parish at the time wanted anything to do with it and so I just faded out of things. But then the associate pastor got a scholarship to Notre Dame and so when he left for Notre Dame the organist asked me to come back and be a cantor. But then the next day he called me and said, after I asked you to come back the pastor called me in and said that Bob Jones was to have no ministerial role in this parish. And so after that my wife and I went to another parish for four years.

It is clear to us that Bob is absorbed by the liturgical perspective and that he moves into the parish with a kind of liturgical vengeance, in that he is immediately involved in several areas of parish life including several liturgical roles. His high liturgical presence, we believe, is why people told him he should become a deacon and why he started at the seminary. However, he has become so disliked that the pastor tells him this is "my Mass not yours." As a consequence, Bob, for all practical purposes, is removed from any liturgical work in the parish. After four years in another parish, Bob returned to St. Olaf's and offered his liturgical services to the new pastor, Fr. Smith, who was in the process of changing parish staff.

Bob: But I wanted to talk to Fr. Smith and see if there was anything I could do so I also gave him one of my papers that I had done for the seminary on the "Role of the Pastor." And I think I gave him a few others to just say to him "this is what I can do." And I think it came off as offending him. Well, soon after he began firing everybody on staff, this was about a year later. Actually, he dismissed all the staff people including the second highest paid musician in the diocese. He had been in the diocese for thirty years, and one year away from full retirement and Smith fires him. See by getting rid of him, Smith will save the Diocese a lot of money. And the whole parish objected to these dismissals but he said look I am the boss here. After he was dismissed the former organist found a job at St. Thomas and there was also a new pastor there. So then I decided to go there and ask the pastor to lunch to ask him if there was anything I could do to help, and to tell him that I was taking classes at the seminary and thinking about the diaconate. He said I think there is and he got me into evangelization. And so I headed up the evangelization committee for three years and I also became a eucharistic minister and a cantor and started writing articles for the bulletin. Boy I'll tell you it was an honor to be published but it was hard writing and coming up with something every week. As I saw it, evangelization encompasses everything in the parish. So I was in everybody's hair. But I still asked if I could be on the council because that is an important body and so I was very active with the staff leadership then as well. And then a woman came into the parish and she started taking theology classes at the seminary and eventually worked her way on as the worship coordinator for the parish and she was on the evangelization committee as well. After a while she became very territorial especially about worship but my thinking was that evangelization also touched on worship but she did not want me to have any say about worship. So she developed some allies and started getting divisive and so one day I was talking to a friend of hers who was on the worship commission and I said to her that she should go to seminary for classes because she could learn a lot down there and bring it back to the parish. And she said like what? And I said, "do you know what are the symbols of the Eucharist?" and she started stumbling around and so I continued and said "now about the bread and the wine" and she said "what about them" and I said why do you bring water up with the bread and wine during the preparation of the gifts?" She didn't know and said something about that is the way the pastor likes it so we do it and so I told her that it conflicts with the symbolism of bread and wine and obscures the symbolism of the important eucharistic symbols, and so this is the kind of knowledge you could bring back to the parish and help the parish. Well she became very offended and said to me well we don't need you and your ideas around here. So then I felt that I did not want to be a part of that divisiveness or war between evangelization and worship and the pastor didn't want to have anything to do with the battle and so I offered my resignation and I quietly faded away there and then out of the parish in 1994.

Again, he rushes in and gets involved. But more importantly, this time he drills a staff person in charge of worship with a battery of liturgical questions about eucharistic symbolism which she cannot answer, and then tells her that she should be taking classes at the seminary. In a sense, he holds her hostage, interrogates her, and then lets her go by saying she and others need more liturgical education. As Erving Goffman might have said, he effaced her face. Bob did not deal with her gently and with respect, and the consequence he created was his own alienation to the point where he resigns and moves on. After spending only a year at St. Thomas, Bob moves on to St. John's parish.

Bob: But I also remembered Fr. Joe and so I went to St. John's and I like the friendliness and coziness of the Mass. But I also kept going to other parishes but I kept coming back to St. John's and in six months I made up my mind and so I asked Fr. Joe out to lunch to ask him if there is anything I could do to help. Well he thought I was a deacon and he said that he didn't need a deacon and I said that I am not a deacon and he couldn't believe it. He said that I thought you were taking me out to ask for a job and I said no I just wanted to help. So he said to me well just look around the parish and whatever it is that you are suppose to do it will come to you. Just listen at meetings and Mass etc. and it will come to you. . . . At the first worship meeting I said hello my name is Bob and I am interested in good liturgy. And so they said we need help with the Easter Vigil and so I helped out with that. So in September of 1996 they asked me if I was coming to the worship meeting and I said I have a class at the seminary and so they said well we'll move the meeting so that you can be there, and that is what they did. Not only that but they asked me to head up the worship commission for the parish. I was suspicious about them asking me to do that but they were straight about it and so that is what I do now.

Mike: What do you do?

Bob: Well, the first year I just listened and observed before making any changes. I wanted to find the sacred cows and I discovered there are a lot of them and I've learned that change is threatening and that it must happen organically not by wholesale fashion. So I observed but I still did teaching at the commission; I taught them and said that the most important thing about liturgy is the principle of the full, active, conscious participation of the faithful in the liturgy and especially to develop the consciousness part of that principle. And I said before we can do that we need to deal with ourselves as the worship commission first and become conscious of what we are doing at liturgy and so at every meeting we will have a prayer service so that they know how to pray and how to do a prayer service and then education of the commission on what is liturgy and then do the business part of the meeting.

Mike: Like what?

Bob: I will show them how to evaluate a liturgy, for example, by looking at the documents on the liturgy not by basing the evaluation on their emotions. That way the change comes from the worship commission not from me or from Fr. Joe and so the worship commission has a voice. So the education follows the liturgy documents not the whim of the people and so that is what I have been doing. . . . When I was visiting parishes and they would have a commitment day for joining commissions I asked a lady who had the worship commission badge on, why do we light that Easter Candle and why are we standing for the eucharistic prayer? And she said we stand because Fr. Joe had a course at Notre Dame and he learned that we are supposed to stand and so we have been standing ever since. And so she went to Fr. Joe and said this man was asking me questions I didn't know how to answer. And so she asked him why do we stand when many parishes kneel? I agreed with him about the standing but his parishioners didn't know why they stood. They stand because it is a prayer of thanksgiving and we stand for thanksgiving, not kneel, we kneel for veneration and adoration. So they are right but they don't know why. And so Fr. Joe came to me and said "well" and then laughed, but now a lot of the people at the parish could tell you why they stand.

Again, Bob gets intimately involved in a number of parish worship activities. In this case, however, he notes that the parish is doing something liturgically correct (standing for the Eucharistic prayer—which is really liturgically incorrect according to the rubrics) but that the people don't understand why they are standing—implying that that is as bad as doing something wrong. Here is a concrete example of what many writers have noted about liturgists and the liturgical movement, namely, that it is overly rationalistic. If people don't intellectually understand why they are doing something at Mass, then it is as bad as doing it incorrectly. The cognitive dimension becomes the basis for critique and ridicule and, as previously noted, the simplest way to move liturgically ignorant people to being liturgically sophisticated and knowledgeable people is through liturgical education. Liturgists have a simple formula for social change—more education. Moreover, for a second time, Bob illustrates the liturgical tactic of interrogation with his many questions. Next we find Bob describing the liturgical issue of the Easter Candle.

> Bob: In his office there is a box with an Easter Candle in it and the pastor lit that every day that he was denied his vows and so that is why he lights the Easter Candle at every Mass and it goes back to this. So I have told Fr. Joe it should be lit only during the Easter season and he said "no I need the light of Christ." And I said, "well the worship commission said we shouldn't light it" and he said "I would be devastated if I didn't light it!" And then I said, "I would appreciate it then if at least during Lent we didn't light it because then how is it important during Easter if it is lit all the time, there would be nothing special about it." Then he said "well I will be devastated but I guess if the worship commission really doesn't want it lit well I will go along with it." At that point he was trying to give me a guilt trip. And so the first Sunday of Lent he removed the candle completely and the people said to me "what did you say to him that he removed the whole candle." So the Easter Candle is a sacred cow. So Fr. Joe does a lot from an emotional level rather than an intellectual one. I mean did you see the tears coming down his face the other day at Mass when he brought that family up with the baby who had surgery and survived? He is like a magnet there (at this point Bob started crying again but not as severely as before). Another sacred cow is that he always carries in the gospel book and I finally said to him that he should not be carrying in the book of gospels and he said to me but I want to. Then a few weeks ago with the new musician he said to me I can't carry in the gospel book because then I wouldn't be able to sing and so he said to me make it happen that someone else carries it in. And so I took it to the worship commission and they agreed and so I wrote an article in the bulletin and so a few months ago the lectors started carrying in the book of the gospels. So now Fr. Joe calls me the "boss of worship."

Bob is slowly becoming an authoritarian liturgist at St. John's as he did in the other parishes. This time he confronts the pastor twice, once about the Easter Candle and the other about the gospel book. But Bob is quick to point out how sensitive he is to others and that he doesn't want to stir up the waters and so he treds lightly, as shown in the next part of the interview. Yet within a year he is running the worship commission and telling the pastor how the liturgy should be conducted.

Bob: But I didn't want to get into divisiveness with Fr. Joe and I learned this from the other parishes I was in and so I tred lightly around these sacred cows. I try to be very careful and so that is how I got the gospel book procedure changed. And so I am continuing to work with the worship commission on liturgical symbols. Another sacred cow is the wine. I don't like the little cups but I can handle the grape juice, I mean it is still fruit of the vine. But this will take some time to change. I'll give you Fr. Joe's take on it and so you will see why it might take some time. He has a strong aversion to drinking out of another's glass first of all and secondly he thinks that alcohol is poison and you don't give children poison or anything like it. And there are a lot of elderly on medication and they can't take alcohol. Also, they have been doing this for fifteen years. Even the regional Bishop came out to talk to him about it but he didn't stop, he still does it. I personally feel a need to bring about a change in this manner of receiving communion but I need to be careful and move slowly because people believe in him and I do not want to disrupt that.

Although Bob says he can accept the grape juice he will soon go to war over this issue, and when he does so he has only been in the parish for two years. He feels well armed with his liturgical knowledge and he has every intention of correcting what he regards as an abusive liturgical situation. And the fact that a bishop had already addressed this issue with the pastor does not deter him or give him pause in the least. But before we get back to the grape juice issue and Bob's tactics for correcting the situation, he has more to say about the role of the worship commission and its relationship to the pastor.

Bob: Music is another thing. The new musician started the third week of September. He is the head of the Metropolitan Oratorial Association and he has a theology and liturgy degree. Also a bachelor's degree in piano and a masters of music and he is presently working on his Ph.D. in music. The parish had a disaster in the area of music when I came and Fr. Joe was really the genesis of it. About three years ago the music director resigned and Fr. Joe hired an eleventh grade prodigy and I knew this kid since he was eight years old. So he was hired and he was there for two years and then he went to college and he wanted to stay and drive home every weekend but that just wouldn't work. Finally this young man said to Fr. Joe, my cantor can do it, who was a young high school girl. Fr. Joe said we had to hire another youth because that is how they can become part of the church more and it encourages them. So here is the junior who knew nothing about liturgy or leadership and she became the new music director and it was a disaster. People started complaining and so I offered to help her and she refused to accept my help, but the people kept complaining and even attendance at Mass started dropping and it was because of the music. And so Fr. Joe finally said this cannot go on and he did not want to hurt her but he finally said to me "go and tell her that she is fired and so I told her that we needed someone who could train children and cantors and who was more available." She right away went to Fr. Joe and he backed me up, finally. And then the mother came in to see me and she said how could you do this to her, she is so depressed and so I just said to her that it was unfair to have hired her in the first place because the parish really wanted more than she was able to give.

Mike: What are some of the other things that you or others dislike about the liturgies?

Bob: Too many announcements, at the end it gets kind of carried away. Some people like the "around the world" prayer for justice and the around the world prayer against violence. But every week it tends to lose its impact, hearing that every week.

Mike: It is done every week?

Bob: Yes, in fact he does it every day. That is why he knows it so well. He goes around the world everyday. And this came about because I think because it was a request from the Justice and Peace Commission. But I think it, it is like repetitive prayer, like the rosary lets say, but after awhile people turn their minds off. So what I'm saying is that it loses its impact. There is some disagreement over how we distribute the wine, and I think traditionalists would like to see it out of the cup because the symbolism is that we all drink from the one cup which we don't do. And this has been the basis of a lot of discussion and, apparently they have been doing it in this parish for some time, and it deals basically with I think a fear that Fr. Joe has of drinking out of the same glass that somebody else does. I mean it is, well I don't know if it is paranoia, but it is very strong. And he has convinced a lot of other people in the community, and its, to me it is one of those battles you can't win, at least at this point in time and so I don't take it up because it is not something—I mean it would cause more alienation than anything. The woman who at the worship commission said that we should let the pastor do whatever he wants, well she is very strongly, adamantly convinced that is what we have to do.

Mike: What else?

Bob: Another thing they do that I think is extremely personable is like the sacraments, like first communion is done individually. Each of the children starting from May through the Summer, they come up during the preparation of gifts and during the eucharistic prayer, they stand at the altar and they stand up there with the priest and years later they remember that, I mean, I have seen how Fr. Joe handles the kids and it is extremely personable. So there is a sense of, this is my priest, and this is Jesus Christ among us. A strong sense of that with the people. However, there is a downside to this. Downside is that everybody wants to run to him for decisions and so this really weakens the structures of the parish. That, well at the council meeting we were discussing how to avoid financial problems by planning the budgets and staying within the budgets and so then the head of the Education Commission says well when I get an idea she says I just go to Fr. Joe and he says to just go ahead with it. So that is the end run that we talked about. The idea at the other end is that you get this personableness but on the other hand you have people running to him to get approval and there are people who walk up to me and say that I would like to do this in worship and I went to Fr. Joe and he has already approved it (laughing). So I am on the receiving end as well.

Mike: So are you saying, why bother having a commission?

Bob: Well, yea. Like the deal with the Easter Candle, if that is already pre—decided then you really don't need a worship commission. And my sense of the worship commission is that it is up to us to assess the worship needs of the parish. We are not there to do what the pastor wants, we are there to identify the worship needs of the parish and then collaborate with the pastor, which is different than finding out what the pastor wants to do and then doing that. And so philosophically he agrees with this but when it comes time to putting it into practice it is not always done. But like a lot of other pastors it is a hard adjustment to make, to this collaborative model.

With the music situation, Bob again is in the midst of the liturgical quagmire, even offering his help to the young musician, who Bob thinks knows nothing about liturgy. He also clearly feels that it is up to the worship commission to assess the worship needs of the community and then assess those needs and implement them. This thinking in Bob's view is purely theoretical, coming out of a collaborative model of ministry, but in actuality it is an oligarchic model. The Vatican II church predisposed many to write and think and even act in a more collaborative way about pastoral decisions making, but the official hierarchical church has not adopted this model as its *modus operandi* – the pastor still makes the decisions. This understanding of church ministry and of the worship commission seems to have eluded Bob. It is interesting to note, however, that in Bob's desire to be collaborative he is being as autocratic as a Vatican I pastor. He himself employs a model of mandated democracy.

The next section of the interview text that we provide illustrates Bob's arrogance, rigidity, and methods of enlightening a fellow parishioner. In this case, Bob interrogates Mary about the meaning of sin and then simply tells her she is doing something wrong. Finally he tells her that she is seriously codependent, with a final dogmatic pronouncement that she "is not to do this anymore."

Bob: Mary is a charismatic and likes to lay hands on anyone she can and she has an eighth grade education and barely lives above the poverty level and she has a lot of strong opinions, but the characteristic one is that she brings communion to the sick and hears their confession. When she told me that I said why are you doing that? Well, because they may want to tell some sins she said. I said, Mary, what do you know about somebody's sins? She said well they feel better after going to confession and so I ask them if there is anything they want to get off their chest. I said Mary you know, if people are asking you for communion they are not in a state of serious sin. Do you have any idea what serious sin is? It means that you have decided to make a change in your fundamental stance in life. And I said that these people who are asking for communion have not made a fundamental change in their stance in life. They are not in serious sin. She said well I just, this is what I always do. See Mike this is serious codependency. So I said well Mary Ann don't do that anymore.

The course of the interview returns to several issues that by now have become more intense and have escalated Bob's conduct. The role of the worship commission, the Easter Candle, Mike withdrawing from the field, Bob's friend

Chris, and, finally, the issue of grape juice for communion instead of wine all resurface. Although Bob has said these issues are divisive and he doesn't want to get into them because they are so divisive, he plunges forward anyway. This time, however, he has gone too far, with the consequence that Fr. Joe removes him from the worship commission (Bob says he also resigned) with the worship commission itself being disbanded for an unknown period of time. Moreover, we believe Bob's removal from the worship commission by the pastor may have motivated him to take further action on the issue of the grape fruit juice because he does so by going to the next level which is the vicar and then finally to the regional bishop as we will see shortly. We begin this segment of the interview with the senior author calling Fr. Joe to inform him of his decision to leave the research site at his parish because Bob has begun using him to legitimize some of his liturgical opinions.

Mike: I am calling to let you know that I am pulling out of the parish as a field researcher.

Fr. Joe: Why is that?

Mike: Because I feel that Bob is deferring to me as some kind of authority in the area of liturgy. One way I think he legitimates what he wants is by deferring to me and I think I am getting caught in a role that I do not want to embrace. I am often shrugging my shoulders when he does that and so I think it best if I leave.

Fr. Joe: Well, its funny you should mention Bob because he just resigned from the worship commission, I just got a letter from him saying so. I just think that Bob is a very needy person. I mean he has been in and out of so many parishes that I thought well I will try to be nice to him and make him feel at home somewhere, I think he needs that and so I have been doing that and then he sends me this letter about the Easter Candle not being lit and people voting at the worship commission against it and then quoting canon law to me. I don't know, he just is very needy and I'm just trying to be pastoral. Well, Mike were you at that meeting?

Mike: Yes I was.

Fr. Joe: And so they voted against that?

Mike: Well, I did not witness any vote. I mean there were people talking, mainly two people talking strongly against it and a couple supporting your lighting it. So I'm not sure what is going on there and he kept looking at me during that meeting and so that made me rethink my presence there.

Fr. Joe: Yes. Well was the other person speaking out against it the heavy woman Chris?

Mike: Yes it was.

Fr. Joe: Well, you know ever since she came on the scene it seems like there has been nothing but trouble. I mean she and Bob have taken some classes at the seminary and now they just seem to have to push those ideas through and I'm trying to be pastoral mainly...Well I am supposed to have dinner with Jack, Sue, and Bob to straighten this out, but I wonder if I should just let it cool down first.

We turn now to an interview segment with Bob where he accounts for why he resigned from the worship commission. Bob does not know that Mike has pulled out from the parish research site.

Bob: I just wanted to let you know that I resigned from the worship commission and I thought you should know about it because of the study.
Mike: What's going on?
Bob: Well you remember the issue about the Easter candle at the worship commission and we voted nine to one and then I wrote the letter to Fr. saying that we are not going to use it anymore and the worship commission backs this, well he used the candle and lit it at Mass and so I had people calling me from the worship commission saying he is lighting the candle and so I resigned—not because of the candle but because he did an end run around the worship commission. And then he wrote an article about the candle and talked about its importance and then he gave a homily on it too and why it is lit and so he is digging his heels in and so now the council is getting involved. And the council is going to say to him, hey, look, you can't do this, you can't just do an end run and pull this authoritarian move. Anyway, Jack, Sue, and Fr. and I are going to have dinner Wednesday night before the worship commission meeting to try and resolve this. Hey, I'm willing to lead the group but if the pastor is going to ignore the worship commission then forget it. I mean even in the last issue of *Liturgix*, the paper out of the worship office, there is an article from a Cardinal on what good liturgy is and there is a list of twenty things in that article that are necessary for good liturgy and we are only doing ten of them! I mean we don't do ten of them. And so I don't want to waste my time. We want Fr. to be part of the worship commission and decision making process but if he is not going to be there and be part of it then he has to abide by what the worship commission decides and its decisions and so he is being authoritarian by not doing what we say and so I don't want to do it anymore. And so anyway I think this is an interesting facet of life in the parish and for the study you are doing, I mean how will this be resolved, and so I wanted to make you aware of this because we will be dealing with it tomorrow. This is part of life in a parish (he is laughing). So are you coming to the meeting?
Mike: I wasn't planning on it.
Bob: Well, it might be interesting for you because you were at the last one and you know the background. So anyway, this is part of the faith journey and about how these kinds of problems get handled. I did see Ralph on Ash Wednesday but I was talking to Jack and Sue about all of this when he came by and so we didn't talk, I mean I was telling Jack and Sue that I was really pissed and they said come sit down with us and I said I'm not going in there, I'm getting out of here and then Jack said, look, let me see what I can do because this really is a parish council issue now, so we will take it up from here and that is why we are having dinner. And so I hope we can resolve this so this kind of thing doesn't fester because I think Father wants the issue to just go away but it is not going to just go away. So I just wanted to let you know.

The next day Fr. Joe called Mike at work to say that he talked with Jack (chairperson of the parish council) and that against his better judgment he has decided to have a dinner meeting with Bob and Jack and Sue. After the dinner he will be going over to the worship commission meeting. The next day after the worship commission meeting and dinner, Bob calls Mike.

Bob: Well, it happened.
Mike: What's that?
Bob: Remember I told you we were having a meeting.
Mike: Yes.
Bob: Well we had it and Fr. Joe has fired me from the commission and he has temporarily withdrawn the worship commission from active duty.
Mike: You mean there is no longer a worship commission?
Bob: That's right, at least for now. He said he will reinstate it later.
Mike: Why?
Bob: Well because he said we did an end run around him with a number of liturgy issues and he didn't appreciate it and he thinks some time off for all involved will give us time to think about what is the worship commission and what is its role as well as a time for all to consider the unique history of this parish.

Bob is angry that Fr. Joe has done an "end run" around the worship commission, yet the worship commission has done an end run around Fr. Joe from his perspective. Moreover, Fr. Joe considers this end run the final straw and suspends the worship commission and Bob from ministry indefinitely. Further evidence of Bob's ingrained sense of righteousness, however, is that he says that the worship commission voted nine to one to remove the Easter Candle at the last worship commission although no such vote took place. What did occur was a discussion about the Easter Candle and Donna, one of the long time members, arguing with Bob about his position. She saw no need to tell Fr. Joe what to do in this situation, "if he wants the candle lit that is good enough for me" she said. This discussion carried on for some time with Donna opposing it vigorously and the remaining members nodding in agreement with Donna but not saying much. Clearly, there is a complete lack of consensus in this situation, out of which Bob again escalates the stakes by going to the vicar and regional bishop. At issue is whether grape juice during eucharist is liturgically correct, as indicated in the next interview segment.

Mike: How are things at the parish?
Bob: Well, a number of things have happened and I've even talked to the Vicar here.
Mike: What did you tell him?
Bob: I told him about the parish using grape juice for wine and that it was unacceptable and against liturgical law and so I just asked for his advice.
Mike: What did he say?

Bob: He told me to go to the regional bishop, and so I called him about it and we'll see.

Mike: Well what did you tell the bishop?

Bob: I told him first of all that I did not want to make this a personal issue, I have nothing against Fr. Joe but that there is a principle involved. I don't want to hurt Fr. Joe or take him on in any way, but that this not drinking real wine was wrong and that something should be done about it. I made it real clear to the bishop that I was not making this a personal issue; it is about the sacred symbols of the liturgy.

Conclusion

Bob is one example of how liturgists tend to behave in the course of attempting to implement their interpretations of Vatican II policies concerning Catholic rituals. While there certainly is variation in how individuals conduct themselves in this regard, we are just as certain that the kinds of issues and tensions revealed in Bob's descriptions are typical and widespread throughout parishes. Again, Greeley portrays that typical conduct in the most unflattering of terms: "Yet the arcane debates, the rubrical nit-picking, the authoritarian (and decidedly uncharming) style of many liturgists, and the prolonged and boring performances that they orchestrate have encapsulated the church's worship in a hard ideological shell."[5] There are a number of interesting issues here.

One issue, as predicted by our theory of policy discussed in Chapter 1, pertains to contextual effects and the indeterminacy of purposeful and rational (or construed as such) action. While Bob has encountered other participants in his various parishes who were not liturgically-ignorant, he seems to have almost completely misunderstood the power of tradition. That is, he fails to grasp that he has been attacking a kind of shadowland of ritual practices that are not rationally understood and framed, but are worship practices that are tied to deep senses of loyalty, moral centering, and habit passed down through families. Rather than attempting to understand those ritual practices, he defines them as forms of deviance and assumes that his liturgical knowledge is the sole solution to what he regards as confused and misguided parish practices. Rational liturgical texts—or what Bob takes them to be—confront traditional practices, and the result was that the parishes' contexts of tradition won out as measured by Bob basically being removed from each and every parish at which he worked and by the fact that he left these parishes more disorganized than when he found them. This kind of liturgical failure raises another interesting issue, namely, what keeps Bob going?

This second issue of persistence and continuity has been addressed in recent work on social movements in terms of collective identity and emotional cultures.[6] Becoming embedded in subgroups of close identification can contribute to the persistence of action, help differentiate group boundaries, and contribute to a kind of oppositional consciousness. These generic processes play out in the case of liturgists, seen as change agents, and especially in terms of their being oppositional insiders insofar as liturgists are involved in cooperative relations with church purposes but conflictual relations with traditional practices. Being thereby met with opposition, Bob and other liturgists persist and tenaciously maintain their strict liturgical perspectives. Conventional identity theory[7] would predict that faced with persistent identity invalidation and opposition, people tend to adjust their identities. Moreover, as Becker and Geer[8] described concerning medical students, there tends to be a loss of idealism as people move along their careers. But neither of these general tendencies seem to occur with most liturgists. Indeed, their idealism tends to remain high over long periods of time.

We think there are two reasons for this persistence. First, much identity theory pertains to situations of mundane everyday life and our common sense understandings about how secular life works. Liturgists, however, are religious workers and thus see themselves operating in arenas of the sacred. Embedded in these arenas, by definition, are the fates of people's souls, and the stakes are perceived as higher than those of mere ordinary life. Accordingly, the tenacity of liturgical perspectives are at least partly driven by the potential consequences of supporting processes of sacralization or desacralization depending on what one allows to occur during liturgical celebrations.

The second reason for the persistence of liturgical idealism is that liturgists tend to be embedded in strong liturgical networks that function as communities of support and emotional culture. They are far more likely than parish or diocesan workers without liturgical training to attend liturgical workshops, belong to liturgical organizations and associations, and attend meetings sponsored by liturgical authorities. As we described in Chapter 3, liturgists engage in an array of bonding mechanisms that support a strict Vatican II interpretation of worship and simultaneously deflect negative liturgical experiences. Moreover, those negative experiences, such as those described in Bob's interview, become the texts of war stories and horror stories told at liturgical meetings and that circulate through liturgical networks. Such stories then become the very rationale to more vigorously maintain their convictions regarding liturgical renewal.

In the coupling of sacred callings and powerful network effects, liturgists such as Bob have difficulty taking the role of others involved in parish work. Liturgists tend to find their own intolerance a virtue, their unveiling of others' liturgical ignorance as educational, their politics as righteous, their disdain as caring, and their failures as successes. These are the experiences that rest inside the situation of the oppositional insider that fuel the authoritarianism Greeley finds so abhorrent. Yet, as they tend to create disorder and some measure of complete chaos, we can see the conditions giving rise to new or altered parish arrangements and thus some measure of social change.

Notes

1. Andrew Greeley, *The Catholic Revolution* (Berkeley: University of California Press, 2004).

2. Greeley, *Catholic Revolution*, 180.

3. From the substantial literature in this area, see W. I. Thomas and Florien Znaniecki, *The Polish Peasant in Europe and America* (Chicago: University of Chicago Press, 1918-20), L. Gottshalk, Clyde Kluckhohn, and Robert Angell, *The Use of Personal Documents in History, Anthropology, and Sociology* (New York: Social Science Research Council, 1945), Roger Barker and Herbert Wright, *One Boy's Day* (New York: Harper and Row, 1951), C. Wright Mills, *The Sociological Imagination* (New York, Oxford University Press, 1959), Daniel Bertaux, *Biography and Society: The Life-History Approach in the Social Sciences* (London: Sage, 1981), Norman Denzin, *Interpretive Biography* (Newbury Park, CA: Sage, 1989), Diane Bjorklund, *Interpreting the Self: Two Hundred Years of American Autobiography* (Chicago: University of Chicago Press, 1998).

4. Barney Glaser and Anselm Strauss, *Time for Dying* (Chicago: Aldine, 1968). A case study applying this concept is found in Anselm Strauss, *Anguish* (San Francisco: The Sociology Press, 1971) and the theoretical underpinning is discussed by G. Riemann and F. Schutze, "Trajectory as a Basic Theoretical Concept for Analyzing Suffering and Disorderly Social Processes," in *Social Organization and Social Processes: Essays in Honor of Anselm Strauss*, ed., David R. Maines (Hawthorne, New York: Aldine de Gruyter, 1991), 333-357. For an overview, see David Maines, "Life Histories and Narratives," in *Encyclopedia of Sociology*, eds. Edgar Borgatta and Rhonda Montgomery (New York: Macmillan, 2000), 1633-9.

5. Greeley, *Catholic Revolution*, 188-9.

6. Jo Reger, "Organizational 'Emotion Work' Through Consciousness-Raising: An Analysis of a Feminist Organization." *Qualitative Sociology* 27 (2004): 205-22.

7. Gregory P. Stone, "Appearance and the Self: A Slightly Revised Version," in *Social Psychology through Symbolic Interactionism*, edited by Gregory Stone and Harvey A. Farberman (New York: Wiley and Sons, 1981); Viktor Gecas and Peter Burke, "Self and Identity" in *Sociological Perspectives on Social Psychology*, eds., Karen Cook, Gary Alan Fine, and James House (Boston: Allyn and Bacon, 1995): 41-67.

8. Howard Becker and Blanche Geer, "The Fate of Idealism in Medical School," *American Sociological Review* 23 (1958): 50-6.

Chapter 5
First Holy Communion

Unlike other Christian denominations, baptism itself into the Catholic faith does not confer full membership in the church. Occurring at infancy, baptism is simply the first ritual in a process of initiation, followed by two succeeding rituals. First holy communion is the second initiation ritual, typically occurring when children are in the second grade, and the final ritual is confirmation, which takes place during high school years. All of these rituals are theologically grounded and are designed to perform some kind of sacred work leading to full Catholic membership. This chapter deals with first holy communion, the second of these rituals, by first discussing the background to how the three rituals together are sequenced and then providing data on how first holy communion was implemented under the influence of Vatican II.

Although the theology of first holy communion had not changed between the Council of Trent (1545-63) and Vatican II, there were a number of changes in pastoral practice during this time that affected the process of Christian initiation. Many dioceses, for instance, decided to develop and implement catechetical instruction for children receiving first holy communion or confirmation (initiation sacraments) following the post-Tridentine emphasis on religious education, which was ignited by the Protestant Reformation to make clear that Catholics were different from Protestants. It was in this socio-religious context that an educational model corresponding to age rather than a sacramental model maintaining the traditional sequence of the sacraments of initiation (baptism, confirmation, eucharist/first communion) was adopted. In eighteenth century France, this model led religious educators to theologically prepare children to receive first holy communion before confirmation. As Maxwell Johnson notes, "Since catechesis itself was oriented more toward the reception of first communion than confirmation, the *Instructions of the Ritual of Toulon* in 1748 stated that: 'in order to be sure that children presented for confirmation in this diocese are adequately instructed, it has been decided that they are to be confirmed only after having received their first communion'.".[1]

Moreover, in 1910, Pope Pius X, still confronted with the defensive cate-chetical concerns for children that followed the Protestant Reformation, issued his famous *Quam singulari* document that underscored and reinforced the pas-toral practice of receiving first communion before confirmation. The Pope clearly stated that first communion should be received at the age of discretion, that is, at the age of seven, effectively moving it from the teen years to second grade. Given that confirmation also was being received at age seven as well, many religious educators postponed confirmation until after first communion by some months and eventually by many years. An underlying pastoral reason for the Pope's decision was because of the widespread Catholic attitude that one should not receive communion because of one's unworthiness, stemming from the rigorist abuses of Jansenism which stressed moral austerity, the sinfulness of the human body, and an elitist notion of salvation. In other words, there was a general Catholic ethos that claimed one was unworthy to receive holy commun-ion unless one received confession/penance first in order to cleanse one's soul. The Pope felt that emphasizing the reception of communion earlier might begin to eliminate such an ethos. Consequently, the educational model of sacramental catechesis and the Pope's concern over Catholics receiving communion led to the disintegration of the reception of the sacraments of initiation in their tradi-tional order. Now, the sequence of initiation rituals was baptism, eucharist (first communion), and then confirmation. The official legislation of the church that articulated the traditional sequence of initiation was largely ignored and confir-mation rapidly became a rite of maturity into full Christian adulthood.

Although the debate over when first communion and confirmation should be received has continued since Vatican II, the pastoral debate over "how to do the ritual" of first communion has intensified and received much more attention at the parish level. Given the overall focus of the book on how policies are inter-preted and implemented at diocesan and parish levels, it is interesting to note that none of the official documents of Vatican II or subsequent liturgical and catechetical documents, including Canon Law, have specifically addressed the ritual enactment of first holy communion. For example, the *Declaration on First Confession and First Communion,* a post-conciliar document, simply reiterates that Pius X's *Quam singulari* should be followed. Similarly, Canon 777:3 states "that children are more fruitfully and deeply instructed through catechetical for-mation after the reception of First Communion." The *Directory for Masses With Children,* another post-Vatican II liturgical document, moreover, has nothing specific to say about the ritual itself. It merely states that "The catechesis prepar-ing children for first communion calls for special mention. In it they should learn not only the truths of faith regarding the eucharist but also how from first com-munion on—after being prepared according to their capacity by penance—they can as full members of Christ's Body take part actively with the People of God in the eucharist, sharing in the Lord's table and the community of their brothers and sisters."[2] And the new *Catechism of the Catholic Church* only mentions the right of children who have been baptized and reached the age of reason to come forward to receive first holy communion. Consequently, what has been contested in terms of first holy communion is how the general principle of active participation should be ritually manifested or implemented. Although theological debates over when first communion should be received continue, the real battle since Vatican II has been over how the ritual is pastorally enacted in local parishes. As we will show, the ritual enactment varies depending on the degree of liturgical influence operative at the parish level and the parents' degree of acceptance of liturgical principles influencing the ritual practice.

Communion as a Contested Situation

First holy communion celebrations prior to and immediately following Vatican II were situations that placed emphasis on the children themselves. Children participated in the ritual celebration together as a class, often they formed a procession around the outside of the church and then walked into the church together, the girls wore white dresses and the boys blue suits, and the Mass was tailored for this occasion. Years after Vatican II and in accordance with the active participation principle, however, children now often participate with their families, they may or may not walk into church together, and they often do not wear the same kind of clothing. Much less emphasis is given to the children *per se*; rather, the entire assembly is emphasized with only some special attention given to the children.

In seeking to implement Vatican II precepts, most liturgists interpreted active participation in terms of the celebration of first holy communion as a situation in which the first communicants should sit with their parents as part of the general assembly rather than having all the children seated together in a special area near the front of the church. That is, there is a specific spatial criterion to the principle. The previous arrangement was perceived as dividing the assembly into special groups, thereby de-emphasizing the entire assembly as the worshiping community and rendering the rest of the assembly as passive spectators. This situation was seen as a direct violation of the policy of full, active, conscious participation of the assembly.

Ron Lewinski, considered a leading spokesperson for the liturgical viewpoint, offered his observations of some first communion celebrations that he attended. At one parish, he observed the following: "led by the cross, the children and their parents entered the church in procession and took their places in the front pews.

Children and parents were seated together." [3] This observation led him to interpret this situation as follows:

> What struck me in this celebration was something very simple: These children were now part of the worshiping assembly that feasts at the table of the Lord. We had just initiated them, embraced them more fully as members of the faithful. We all knew it was a special day for the children, yet this never drew our attention away from what we were there to celebrate together: the mystery of Christ's sacrifice and our common sharing in the table of the Lord.

This description mirrors how many liturgists define the situation of active participation with respect to first holy communion. He contrasts the situation above with one involving children and families sitting apart, which he presents as illustrating liturgical insufficiency:

> There was so much attention given to the children and so much effort put into making the occasion "special" that the liturgy felt like a graduation exercise from a catechetical program or a religious pageant performed for the benefit of parents and grandparents. The larger assembly was left behind as passive observers.[4]

While Lewinski concludes that making this celebration special for the children reduced the role of the assembly to that of spectators, many parents do not interpret the above passage as a situation in which the rest of the assembly is transformed into passive spectators. Nevertheless, liturgists insist that it does lead to passive spectatorship and is therefore in violation of a fundamental liturgical principle legitimized by the Second Vatican Council.

The liturgical principle of active participation also has been widely discussed at the national level, especially in the meetings of the Federation of Diocesan Liturgical Commissions (FDLC), which votes on position statements that eventually are placed on the agenda of the National Conference of Catholic Bishops (NCCB renamed in 2002 as USCCB). In these FDLC deliberations, "active participation" is strongly invoked as the rationale for a variety of position statements. For instance, the senior author, who attended the FDLC national meeting in October 1994, heard the principle of "active participation" in most of the major presentations as well as in most of the floor discussions. It seemed as if this policy was the group's ritual incantation bringing about collective effervescence, social solidarity and identity (as described in chapter 3 as well). Indeed, when the position statement "Catechetical Commentary for the Rite of Marriage" was on the floor for discussion, a woman from the Sacramento Diocese exhorted about how couples today preparing for marriage have no sense of the principle of active participation as it relates to marriage, but instead have pagan and superstitious attitudes toward the sacrament of marriage. When finished, she was applauded.

The principle of active participation is promulgated and promoted at the national level by liturgists who expect it to then travel down to the diocesan level and finally to the parish level. But it is not a smooth ride. Exactly what Vatican II meant in practical terms by the policy of active participation remains unclear. Especially at the local parish level, as we will see, there frequently is little consensus regarding the definition of the situation of this policy and that dissensus can affect the practice of first holy communion in dramatic ways.

Data and Methods

Our research site was a parish that we call St. Catherine's, which is located in the suburbs of the Detroit Archdiocese. It is typically suburban, consisting of white, middle class people, with approximately 1200 families and an average age of 45. About 150 children go through their first holy communion ceremony each year.

Like all parishes, the people of St. Catherine's had to interpret and apply the principle of active participation to their worship and other parish activities. For several years prior to our involvement in the parish, that principle had been applied in an inconsistent way that stemmed from a variety of strong opinions. The result was that, in the words of a parish member, first holy communion celebrations had come to have "circus-like" qualities to them. Accompanying the rather chaotic attempts to implement the principle was a widespread dissatisfaction among parishioners and parish officials alike, all of whom felt that holy communion was not sufficiently defined and ritual-like.

As a consequence of this problematic situation, the parish Director of Religious Education announced that an open meeting would be held and a subcommittee formed to address the concern of parents and parish officials. Sixteen parents and parishioners, fourteen women and two men, volunteered to serve on the subcommittee, which also included the Director of Religious Education, her assistant, and the associate pastor. This committee met for six months and discussed a range of issues pertaining to the question of how to conduct the rite of first holy communion in accordance with the principle of active participation. Among all the issues discussed, the one that generated the most heated debate was whether the children would sit together as a group or with their parents. This spatial dimension became the *de facto* demarcation criterion for whether parishioner participation was active or passive and, therefore, whether the parish was implementing the intentions of the church policy.

Our data were collected in the mid-1990s, and are based on participant observation and interviewing procedures. We attended the subcommittee meetings on three different occasions, the national FDLC meeting once, and the regional meeting (Michigan and Ohio representatives) of the FDLC once. In these subcommittee meetings, discussion was initiated by a professional pastoral minister, liturgist, or Director of Religious Education who made a formal presentation to the committee and framed the discussion. Critical data were collected at the last meeting where all committee members voted on whether or not the children would sit with their family for the ceremony. These are important and provocative data because of how the vote was taken. Sitting in a semi-circle with a black board at the open end, each person not only voted but expressed why they voted the way they did. As the vote was taken, the chairperson jotted down on the blackboard the vote and a summary of each person's rationale.

These observational data were supplemented by interviews with key participants. We interviewed the Director of Religious Education four times, once after each of the presentations to the subcommittee and once a couple of weeks after the last meeting when the committee voted. These interviews focused on what the Director of Religious Education understood to be correct liturgical practices as envisioned by Vatican II's Constitution on the Sacred Liturgy. Several times the principle of active participation was underscored by the Director of Religious Education to justify the measures she wanted implemented in the celebration of first holy communion. Repeatedly, the notion of the assembly and their full, active, and conscious participation was mentioned as a justifying vocabulary of motive.

We conducted informal interviews with parents throughout the process as well. These interviews focused on how the parents felt about the changes in first holy communion practices, how the children were affected by the changes, and what the principle of active participation meant to them. Finally, we attended and observed one of the two liturgies of first holy communion in order to document what ideas or suggestions from the meetings were actually put into practice.

With these data, we can address the question of how this particular parish defined the situation that confronted it by virtue of changes in church policy discussed in Vatican II's Constitution on the Sacred Liturgy. We will present data that indicate the decision-making processes of the subcommittee, and will focus sharply on the core issue of seating arrangements. As will be described, a considerable fracture in interpretation of the principle of active participation emerged between the parents and the parish officials.

Findings

We found that both parish professionals and parents were dissatisfied with how first holy communion had been celebrated in the past several years, which led eventually to the formation of the subcommittee. As previously mentioned, professionals and parents defined the celebration as "circus-like," meaning that the ritual did not flow smoothly. Both groups defined the ritual as chaotic, which meant that not only was the flow of the ritual choppy but it consequently was insufficiently sacred. There were two areas of activity that led to this dissatisfaction: people with cameras taking pictures, and the children moving out of their seats to go to the front of the church.

Picture Taking

It was unanimous among the parents and professionals that the picture taking had gotten out of hand. Parents and other family members were not only taking pictures during their child's reception of first holy communion but throughout the entire ritual. It seemed as if every time the children physically moved or even opened their mouths to pray or sing cameras started going off, many with flashes. As one parent mentioned, "having a few pictures taken isn't so bad, but throughout the entire Mass is just too much, especially if the cameras have flashes. It looks like a circus or something." The DRE and associate pastor agreed. The associate pastor stated that "the camera taking simply detracts from the sacramental dimension of the celebration, especially all of the flashes. I felt like I was at a school play rather than the liturgy of the eucharist." Indeed, the entire committee agreed to prohibit the use of cameras during the celebration of first holy communion. In order to appease parents and other family members and friends, however, the committee decided to hire a professional photographer to take a picture of each child receiving their first holy communion. The photographer was to be inconspicuous, and the celebration would thereby flow more smoothly, and thus contribute to the solemnity of the celebration.

Movement of Children

Another major problem pertained to the movement of the children during the celebration. Specifically, during the Eucharistic Prayer, the children moved from their pews and walked to the front of the church and gathered around the altar with the priest. The main problem with this was that the children were seated with their parents who were scattered throughout the church. Thus, when it came time for the children to gather around the altar, kneelers were lifted thunderously, hymnbooks were dropped, children hopped over the laps of parents, some returning to their pew to return their hymnbook because they had forgotten to do so a minute earlier, most scurried about rather than solemnly walking to the altar, and once they got to the front, the priest had to take the role of an usher and arrange each child in order to obtain some semblance of order. Moreover, as they proceeded forward, cameras began flashing throughout the church. One parent exclaimed: "the craziest time in the liturgy was when the children gathered around the altar. I mean it was nuts; noise, kids, cameras, coughing, sneezing, talking. It was chaos." Again, the professionals agreed. The associate pastor felt that the song accompanying their procession forward just added to the chaos and confusion, and felt that deleting the song from the ritual might help: "Children could gather around the altar during the Eucharistic Prayer, but without fanfare and singing. Simply walking up and circling the altar is the symbol which speaks for itself! Thus, no gathering song." The parents and professionals, therefore, were in agreement over the fact that something had to be done. The disagreement, of course, was over what exactly should be done.

During the committee meetings, therefore, several issues arose over how to enact the ritual of first holy communion so as to render it special, sacred, and ritual-like. The two issues in particular that became central to their discussions were the singing of the prayer called the "Our Father" and peer-seating. Although peer-seating generated the most debate, the singing of the Our Father consumed much of the committee's time and energy. We therefore will briefly describe this issue before moving to the main points of contention.

Our Father

Two of the parents were volunteer catechists in the Religious Education Program of the parish, and were told during their training for this position that there were a number of books available to assist them in their preparation for teaching. One book suggested teaching the children a particular version of the Our Father that was not officially approved by the church, unbenounced to the parent/catechists. When the parents wanted the children to sing this version of the Our Father during the first communion celebration, the professional staff strongly suggested that it should not be used. For example, the associate pastor noted: "The Our Father should be the version prescribed in the *Sacramentary* (the book the priest uses at the altar during Mass), not the song about the Our Father that was used [in previous years]."
In response, the parent/catechists explained that "the children practiced this song all year long so they would be able to sing it at their first holy communion and sing it well. I don't see why that is such a problem. It makes the celebration a little more special for the children." At that point, one of the professional guest speakers at the meeting spoke up: "the Our Father is one of those prayers that everyone knows and can participate in fully. To use a children's version of the prayer would deprive the rest of the assembly of a key moment in which to participate fully and actively."
A parent responded, "yeah, but again, it is only once a year and so I don't see why it would be so bad, why the rest of the people would be so uninvolved. In fact, it is easy to sing and the people could probably pick it right up." The professional guest speaker responded: "but it is one of those universal kind of prayers that even non-Catholics can pray. There seems to be so few prayers we can all join in on together that we should at least try to maintain the integrity of this prayer." The DRE then supported the guest speaker by saying: "The International Commission for English

on the Liturgy spent ten years discussing the appropriate version of the Our Father that should be used at Mass, and so I don't think we have the authority to say 'oh well let's use this one, it sounds nice.' The sacramentary is our touchstone and we should respect it." One of the parents then said, "well, why were we given this textbook then? We were told to use these books to help us in our teaching. Now we can't use something we have been using all year long. That doesn't make sense." The DRE responded then by saying: "I have only been here a year and I didn't know that song was in the text. I should look into that more. But still it isn't the best and we should consider being more faithful to the sacramentary."

The discussion continued for a while longer and then it was decided to move onto the question of peer-seating with the hope of coming back to the question of the Our Father. Nevertheless, parents and officials were at odds over this particular aspect of the ritual. As the meetings proceeded, though, the parents tacitly conceded issues such as the Our Father in order to devote most of their energy to the issue of peer-seating. We now present a more detailed ethnographic description of the committee meetings and the discussion of peer seating by first presenting how the professionals defined the situation of peer-seating and second how the parents defined it.

Professionals' Views of Peer Seating

At the very outset of these meetings, the professional staff decided to have the sub-committee read various liturgical articles[5] pertaining to first communion as well as to host three evening meetings where experts in liturgy and religious education were invited to speak. The basic text or document that the professionals utilized in presenting their views was the policy or principle of the full, active, conscious participation of the faithful found in the Constitution on the Sacred Liturgy. In interpreting this principle, they followed the line of reasoning that Fr. Ron Lewinski proposed in his interpretation of child/peer seating as a situation that reduced the remaining assembly to mere spectators. Repeatedly, the professionals emphasized the primacy of the assembly and that everything done in the liturgy should ensure their full participation. This perspective was born out in a memo about first holy communion from the associate pastor to the DRE which stated:

> At no time during the Liturgy of the Eucharist should the children stand in front of the altar, or at the Presider's microphone. There should be no songs done by the children only; during any part of the Liturgy; the whole congregation must participate.

All activity should not stop on the Communion of the children at the Communion Rite. [The congregation should commune together at Sunday eucharist.]

The Communion song(s) should be participated in by all not by just the children. It should be led by the cantor or organist, [Liturgically] speaking, not the children. "Magnificat" and "His Banner Over Us is Love" was not liturgically appropriate since the congregation could not join in the singing. This is not a recital or school play–it is the Liturgy of the Eucharist! Moreover, "His Banner Over Us is Love" completely replaced the Prayer After Communion. This is absolutely incorrect.

Given that liturgical position, peer seating was interpreted as a detraction from full assembly participation. As the DRE stated throughout the many meetings and in conjunction with the associate pastor's many comments in his memo (see above), "the whole religious education program is family focused and it encourages family participation. And so the family should be with the kids. If not, they become like spectators." The DRE on other occasions reiterated that the liturgical focus needs to be on the entire congregation and that less focus should be placed on the children:

If we focus on the children in this celebration, where will it end? Next week some other group in the parish will want the liturgy to focus on their group like the girl scouts or boy scouts or young singles or elderly or married couples. It could get to the point where every Sunday we are focusing on a special group, leaving the assembly passive. The whole point of the principle of active participation is that the whole congregation participate not special groups within the congregation.

In an issue of *Church*, a major liturgical journal that is received by parishes, the chair of the National Catechetical Renewal Network, expressed this same perspective:

At each first Communion liturgy, reserve as many seats up-front as necessary and invite the children to sit with their families. Guide the youngsters to receive Communion not as a subgroup, lined up with their peers, but to take their turn along with everyone else.

Make sure the ushers understand what is to take place and why so they will be prepared to orchestrate the Communion line, pew after pew, just as at any Sunday liturgy. Receiving the eucharist with and among the whole community signifies the child's Communion with the adult church.

Be forewarned! The congregation might find this unusual arrangement uncomfortable, and some ushers have even found it difficult not to group the first communicants together at the head of the line.[6]

Yet another expression of this perspective was articulated by Dr. Elaine Rendler, who is a regular on the National Liturgical Speaker's Circuit. In a talk given in Detroit she made the following remarks:

> Regarding first holy communion; it's a major thing to suggest to people that we move it from a special celebration on Saturday to a regular Sunday celebration.
> In one parish in Washington the children dress up and that's not a bad idea but all the children were seated up front together and their parents were way in the back behind them. This just doesn't work. They are suppose to be a family and so they should sit together and besides the parents should be thanked first because most don't have faith.[7]

Other data reflecting the professional's point of view were obtained during one of the regional meetings of the FDLC, in which thirteen liturgists discussed the issue of peer-seating. Their views were similar to those stated above, except that their responses were filled with emotional disdain for the practice of peer-seating, no doubt reflecting the collective disdain for deviations from liturgical norms that characterizes these gatherings. In fact, a kind of disdainful emotional mood seemed to spread through the group as their discussion unfolded. Indeed, the use of the term "kiddy liturgy" captured their disdain as the following responses to field interviews show:

> We have them sit with their family, that is where they really belong, otherwise it turns into a kiddy liturgy.

> We do the family approach too. And we try to get away from special songs for these quote special kids etc., because then it is not the assembly's prayer, but these kids' prayer and we are back to kiddy liturgies. The family approach then helps you move away from kiddy liturgies, you know, kiddy songs, kiddy prayers, kiddy homilies.

> We do all 100 kids together at a special liturgy on Saturday but it is too kiddy focused even though most parishes have them sit with their families. We are trying to move toward what someone mentioned earlier about having smaller groups of kids and parents celebrating together. But many tell me, as is the case in my own parish, that the parents say No because this has been the tradition here to have a special liturgy. But it is terrible, kiddy this and kiddy that.

> We have the same problem, even worse in that all the 100 kids have a ministry during the liturgy–it is absolutely ridiculous. Many will read one or two lines of a prayer or of a reading, or they will bring up a flower and place it by the altar–others will bring a flower to their mother. It is just all these kids doing stuff during the liturgy and it is kid focused, it's terrible.

We have the same kiddy liturgy problem. But why are the kids doing the readings when their catechists should be doing this given that they have been teaching them about God's word all along and have been proclaiming it to them supposedly?

We too have the kiddy problem. But the problem is, what are we saying about the theology of the assembly when all of this kiddy stuff is going on? So I think it is better when they are in the assembly. All these special things they do are just foolish.

Parents' Views of Peer Seating

The parents' responses to this policy were at first mixed and slow to emerge, but eventually their responses became straightforward and clearly reflected their ability to assimilate and articulate to their advantage the principle of active participation. For example, at the second to last meeting of the sub-committee, the Director of Religious Education repeated her "family focus" theme, and one parent immediately responded that "these kids are with their families every Sunday all year round. This is a special day and it is a personal day, and so not being with the family will not make me a spectator. I will be watching and praying." Another parent supported this viewpoint by saying, "my son seated with the rest of his class will not make me a passive spectator. I will still participate, singing songs and saying the prayers and especially watching my son."

Many of the responses that advocated peer seating, however, were based on practical reasoning rather than interpretation of family togetherness. Here parents argued, for example, that the children would be able to see better if they sat with one another. Many of the parents referred to the first communion celebrations of the past two years, and stated strongly that the children simply could not see because they were seated behind an adult. Moreover, a few utilized the above statement to argue that if the children are able to see, then active participation would be more likely to occur. As one parent said: "it is easier to handle logistically and also the kids can relate better. And of course they can see better."

Other responses from the parents, however, pertained directly to issues of peer group solidarity. For instance, one parent argued that "they are going to class together and so they are being initiated as a group and going through a good deal of their life together as a group and so they should sit together." Several of the parents asked their children about the seating arrangements, and they reported that 95 percent of the children said they wanted to sit with their class rather than with their parents. Others felt that having the children sit together made the occasion special. As another parent stated; "My son feels more special when sitting with his peers. It is a little different than normal Sunday Mass."

And finally there were two parents who emphasized their children's individual decision to sit with their friends and go through communion without their family. For example, "I want peer seating because my son is making his first communion, not the family. I am proud of him to be able to confidently and independently go up to the altar on his own and make his first communion and I will be able to see him do it." Another woman said something similar: "It is something special with Jesus, and the reverence just isn't there when they sit with their parents. My son has to develop this bond with Christ himself. This is his individual choice and I'm proud of that, so he should go up on his own."

Liturgists frown on such attitudes on the grounds that the liturgy by its nature is public and communal, not individualistic. Placing such an emphasis on the individual, liturgists believe, detracts from the full, active participation of the entire assembly. As the Director of Religious Education stated in response: "But you must remember that the liturgy is a communal celebration of the whole assembly; it is not just those making their first holy communion." That argument did not convince the parents to change their minds, and at the end of six months of study and discussion, the sub-committee decided to vote on the seating arrangement and the parents prevailed: all sixteen parents voted for peer seating, and the two professionals voted for family seating.

We have interpreted this vote as a sign of the parent's growing dissatisfaction with the professional's definition of full, active, conscious participation and, indeed, their ultimate rejection of this principle as it pertains to the celebration of first holy communion. In discussing the vote with the DRE the following week, we discovered that while the professionals were discouraged by the vote, they nevertheless would abide by the decision. As the DRE reflected on the experience, she said: "I was disappointed in that we were trying to present what Vatican II said about the sacraments and how Catholics need to absorb a more communal approach to the sacraments, not an individualistic one like in the past." We asked her at that point if that is why the professionals spent so much time emphasizing the principle of active participation:

Yes. The very essence of the principle is that the community is most important in the liturgy not individuals. The liturgy is not the time for individual, private prayer or a time to focus just on individual groups. The entire assembly or congregation is the symbol of the Body of Christ. The Catholic church is trying to move away from a private understanding and celebration of the sacraments. And the principle of active participation embodies that notion. And so I am disappointed in that the people didn't understand that.

Conclusion

The policy we have examined, namely the Vatican II principle that mandates the full and active participation of the faithful, was a broad one that lacked definitive markers or criteria for implementation. Like all policies, it was a set of intentions that sought to push change in a particular direction, and it broadly defined what constitutes proper conduct and attitudes among Catholics. Embedded in Canon Law, it has existed as a set of guidelines for the revision of a wide array of standard Catholic practices. These areas can be thought of as the horizontal axis of change that maps the breadth of the policy-implementation process. While we have only touched on this dimension, we have focused more sharply on the vertical axis, which maps the translation of policy in one area (first communion) through hierarchically-arranged groups, with our specific interest being in how one local parish dealt with the policy. Therefore, while we cannot speak to issues pertaining to the extent of implementation, we can speak to what it means to constituent groups in terms of their concrete actions taken to carry out or deflect the policy. In the case of the parish we studied, parish members were faced with several practical issues that were implicated in the Vatican II precept.

The overriding issue facing the parish was how to translate church policy into action. This issue, of course, is a generic one in all cases of policy change, but in the instance of the St. Catherine's Parish, it pertained to how participants were to construct the rite of first communion in light of Vatican II policies. Parish members had to answer questions of what they would do in concrete behavioral terms and what that behavior would mean. The answers to those questions took well over a year and involved a number of tacit concepts which were problematic and contributed to the implementation's contested qualities. Especially problematic was the concept of "active participation": what are parish members to do when they are "active" and when they "participate"? And, if they actively participate, will their actions produce the community solidarity among the full assembly envisioned by the authors and promoters of the liturgical principles?

Our data show that the parish dialogue concerning these issues flowed along a substantial split that configured what George Herbert Mead would have regarded as a problematic future.[8]   On the one hand, the parish officials adopted the strict liturgical view that active participation meant that parents and children must sit together and that the community of the faithful would be symbolized if not actually produced through such action. This viewpoint is very consistent with suburban parishes in general insofar as officials overwhelmingly tend to make denotative interpretations of church policy.[9] They also tend to take a more cognitive and analytical approach to interpreting the meaning of policy, as illustrated in the St. Catherine's case when the parish officials used the presentation format and liturgical analyses in advocating their position.

On the other hand, the parents strongly felt that their children should sit together as a group separate from the adults. Their rationale was practical (the children could see better and thus more actively participate) and was grounded in mundane common sense (the children should sit with their friends and thus with an already-existing community). They also expressed an ironic individualism–that they, as parents, could feel close and bonded to their children by merely watching them, and also be proud of their children because they are enacting their first communion on their own and without their parents.

The fact that the parents' definition of active participation was voted into actual practice suggests some interesting points. First, the split between the parish officials and the parents may well not be that unusual. Indeed, scholars have noted that an increasingly educated and organizationally-oriented clergy in American religion has contributed to a gulf between themselves and the ordinary pew dweller.[10] Douglas in particular lays the blame on the professionalization of the clergy. As she has written, "It is as if the liturgical signal boxes were manned by color-blind signalmen."[11] Second, the process and outcome of the parish vote are consistent with what Stephen Warner [12] calls "*de facto* congregationalism." By that, he means that the local church is more effectively constituted by its members than by territory or authority relations within the denomination. *De facto* congregationalism implies a conflation of the expressive nature of worship and the instrumental nature of policy decision-making, as congregations themselves move to take on a measure of formal responsibility in the determination of forms of worship, although this formal responsibility appears to be focused on more local group solidarity issues than on the broader scope of the professionals.

Related to these two issues is a third one that pertains to the effects of Vatican II at the parish level. One of the major effects has been a degree of democratization of the church, since under Vatican I the parents of St. Catherine's would not even have had an opportunity to discuss liturgical policy and vote on its implementation. Beyond that, though, the effects are mixed. The parents voted in the Vatican I element of the children sitting together as a class, but they did so on the grounds of Vatican II principles of parishioner empowerment and on secular grounds. Parish members tailored the policy to fit themselves, as it were, and they created a first communion ritual with which they felt comfortable but still was recognizable as a ritual. At the base of that configuration of ritual was a secular conception of community, a network of weak ties, and an existing family solidarity that was used as the rationale for the position taken in interpreting the policy of active participation. In that view, the age and spatial segregation that is intrinsic to American social structure was not defined as a threat to group solidarity, but rather as one of the foundations of it. Thus, the viewpoint the parents actually voted against was one that they regarded as artificial and as counter productive to the goal of active participation.

Finally, we emphasize again that policies are similar to all rule structures and normative orders insofar as they constitute the frameworks for actual behavior but do not in themselves cause human conduct. Policies may well originate in powerful decision making groups, but they must flow through contexts and networks of relations in order to have any effects.[13] In flowing through those contexts, they invariably are changed to one degree or another, depending on the properties and characteristics of the contexts themselves. That change is put in motion through people confronting one another with their interpretations of the policy in an attempt to develop meaningful situations of solidarity that are suggested in the policy's intentions. In this sense, policy implementers are also policy makers, which is exactly what the parents of St. Catherine's became.

Notes

1. Maxwell E. Johnson, *The Rites of Christian Initiation: Their Evolution and Interpretation* (Collegeville: The Liturgical Press, 1999), 298.
2. *Directory for Masses With Children*, paragraph 12.
3. Ron Lewinski, "Celebrating First Communion," *Liturgy 90* (January, 1990), 10.
4. Lewinski, "Celebrating", 11.
5. Articles the subcommittee was asked to read included Tim Dornfeld, "Rethinking Children's Liturgy of the Word," *Modern Liturgy* (21: 1994): 14-16; Gael Gensler, "The Rite of Christian Initiation Adapted for Children: First Steps," *Catechumenate* (May , 1990),:15-19; John-Brooks Leonard, "Children of the Promise: A Place in the Assembly," *Assembly* (17: 1991):524-6; Ron Lewinski, "Celebrating," 10-15. It should be noted that these were not primary Vatican II texts but liturgists' interpretations of Vatican II intentions.
6. Judith Dunlap, "First Communion: A Teachable Moment," *Church* (Spring 1995), 44.
7. Elaine Rendler, "Liturgy 2000," (a paper presented to the Department of Parish Life, Archdiocese of Detroit, May 1995).
8. For a discussion of problematic futures, see David Maines, Noreen Sugrue, and Michael Katovich, "The Sociological Import of G. H. Mead's Theory of the Past," *American Sociological Review* 48 (1983): 151-73.
9. See Michael J. McCallion, *The Rite of Christian Initiation of Adults in City and Suburban Parishes in the Archdiocese of Detroit* (Doctoral Dissertation: Wayne State University, 1996).
10. For instance, Mary Douglas, *Natural Symbols, Explorations in Cosmology* (New York: Vintage Books, 1970) and Barbara Hargrove, "Religion, Development, and Changing Paradigms," *Sociological Analysis* 49 (1988): 33-48.
11. Douglas, *Natural Symbols, 62*
12. Stephen Warner, *"Work in Progress: Toward a New Paradigm for the Sociological Study of Religion in the United States,"* *American Journal of Sociology* 98 (1993): 1044-93.

13. On network effects, see Gary Alan Fine and Sherryl Kleinmann, "Network and Meaning: An Interactionist Approach to Structure" *Symbolic Interaction* 6 (1983): 97-110.

Chapter 6
The Rite of Christian Initiation of Adults

This chapter examines the liturgical policies of the Rite of Christian Initiation of Adults (RCIA), which is a set of rituals that constitute a status passage for non-Catholic adults who want to become Catholic. Unlike first holy communion that we examined in the last chapter, those who pass through the RCIA receive all of the sacraments of initiation at the same time during the celebration of the Easter Vigil. In other words, they are made full members of the church at this one liturgical celebration rather than receiving baptism, confirmation, and eucharist at separate times.

We will examine how liturgical professionals play a pivotal role in determining how Vatican II policies pertaining to RCIA will be implemented at the parish level. We discovered that those parish staff professionals who were strongly connected to liturgical social networks and/or had strong liturgical training and background are more likely to narrowly interpret and implement the policies of the RCIA, while those less connected to the liturgical social network tend to interpret and implement the policies more broadly. As it so happens, those narrowly implementing the RCIA policies are in suburban parishes and those broadly implementing these same policies are in city parishes. Consequently, geographical location and strong connections to the liturgical social networks are important variables to consider in terms of how the RCIA is implemented in local parish situations. We first present a short history of the RCIA and the policies of the RCIA as Vatican II mandated them, our data and methods, and then how these new church professionals called RCIA coordinators interpret and implement these policies at the local parish level.

Short History of the RCIA

The RCIA goes back to the early centuries of the church, and originally involved a guided process normally lasting three years through which people internalized the church's entire worldview of faith by living in a Christian community. Christians in those early days were made, not born[1], and because of Christian persecution, the church wanted to construct a rigorous and intensive process to ensure high commitment. This process, which later became known as the catechumenate, reached its apex in the fourth to sixth centuries that Searle refers to as "the Classical era of Christian initiation."[2]

After the sixth century, the rite of initiation went into a long period of decline and disintegration until the Second Vatican Council. The decline stemmed from a number of factors, such as the increasing practice of infant baptism, bishops reserving the right to confirm and not allowing priests to confirm, theological disputes over the similarities and differences between baptism and confirmation as well as socio-political developments. Up to the sixth century, for example, all the sacraments of initiation (baptism, confirmation, and eucharist) were celebrated together, but for a variety of geographic, demographic, and theological reasons,[3] they gradually began to be celebrated separately thereafter. By the Middle Ages, the rite of initiation merely entailed a local priest asking applicants a few questions, baptizing them, and then declaring them Catholics. For all practical purposes, it had withered away into a localized, semi-private perfunctory ritual between priest and candidate.

The Vatican II liturgical commission that drafted the Constitution on the Sacred Liturgy was unanimous in wanting to restore the catechumenate. The policy intention is stated in paragraph 64 of the Constitution:

> The catechumenate for adults, comprising several distinct steps, is to be restored and brought into use at the discretion of the local ordinary. By this means the time of the catechumenate, which is intended as a period of suitable instruction, may be sanctified by sacred rites to be celebrated at successive intervals of time.[4]

This policy, written in 1964, is a general one that only mandates the restoration of the catechumenate as a series of sacred rites, but still gives each parish the option of activating the rite or not. The implementation procedures were left to the work of a post-conciliar commission that finished its work and issued its edition of the RCIA, which was translated almost immediately into English for use in the United States in 1974. The RCIA now specified three rituals marking off four time periods. During the Pre-catechumenate (period 1), people expressed interest in becoming Catholic. This is a period of inquiry and discussion with priests, pastors or RCIA coordinators as well as visiting the parish. If they decide to enter the process of initiation, they participate in the Rite of Acceptance (first ritual marking), which transforms them from inquirers into catechumens, which consequently marks the beginning of the second period called the catechumenate. After a lengthy period of catechetical formation or learning during the catechumenate period, the Rite of Election (second ritual marking) is celebrated which transforms the catechumens into the "Elect." This ritual celebration also begins the third period of the RCIA called The Enlightenment period. This is a period of intense spiritual formation for those elected to receive the sacraments of initiation at the Easter Vigil only six weeks away. After this period of spiritual formation, the Elect go through the rites of initiation (baptism, confirmation, and eucharist) at the Easter Vigil which transforms them into Catholics. This last ritual celebration is the beginning of the fourth period named "Mystagogia" in which the new Catholics are referred to as neophytes–the newly initiated. The period of mystagogia is suppose to last approximately one year so that the neophytes have the opportunity to delve more deeply into the sacred mysteries of Christ experienced at Easter and in the church at large. Each period intensifies the conversion process and allows the initiates to discern their calling to faith. Each step in the process involves a public liturgical ritual that takes place in the midst of the community, publicly marking the initiate's progress.

These periods and steps constitute the church's official policy of adult initiation, becoming mandatory in the United States in 1988.[5] Parishes as of 1988, therefore, no longer had the option of using the RCIA or not. But one of the most telling policies, because each and every RCIA coordinator struggled with it, is number six of The National Statutes for the RCIA in the United States which reads:

> The period of the catechumenate, beginning at Acceptance into the Order of Catechumens and including both the catechumenate proper and the period of purification and enlightenment after election or enrollment of names, should extend for at least one year of formation, instruction, and probation. Ordinarily this period should go from at least the Easter season of one year until the next; preferably it should begin before Lent in one year and extend until Easter of the following year.[6]

This policy clearly addresses the temporal ordering of initiation with which all RCIA coordinators had problems in one way or another, as we will discuss in detail below. But it is helpful to point out that the assumption of this policy is that those adults wishing to become Catholic are not connected or have little connection to the local Catholic parish. Sociologically speaking these candidates lack a sense of gemeinschaft or community, and this policy assumes that it will take at least one year to instill such a sense of community. The RCIA is formally regarded as a kind of sacred temporal order, therefore, involving covenantal relations[7] designed to produce either identity conversion or alternations, in Travisano's terms,[8] depending on the prior religious faith of the person involved. The primary metaphor of the RCIA is that of a journey, with stages representing points of passage along its course and the destination being a new Catholic who is able to experience and articulate the presence of Christ in the spiritual community.

The church has recognized the difficulty, however, in assessing progress and movement through the RCIA. And although neither the Vatican II documents nor the RCIA document itself specifies whether or not each parish should employ an RCIA coordinator, the church generally and local parishes specifically recognized the need for someone to oversee the process of initiation in order to help guarantee its implementation as well as to ensure the integrity of the RCIA itself. Although the RCIA does mention the different ministries involved in the RCIA, such as bishop, priest, sponsors, and the local community, it does not specify exactly who should be responsible for the overall coordination and implementation of the RCIA other than the pastor. Consequently, the church developed the ministry of the RCIA coordinator, and numerous workshops and liturgical events at national and diocesan levels were conducted to train these RCIA coordinators. In many parishes this ministry was combined with the Director of Religious Education's job description or the liturgist's job description (if the parish had such a person), and in a few parishes full or part-time RCIA coordinators were hired. What was clearly evident, then, was the naming of some person to be the RCIA coordinator and to oversee the RCIA's overall implementation at the parish level.

Data and Methods

We draw on two sets of data in this chapter. The first is a social survey of RCIA coordinators in the Detroit Archdiocese, and the second is a set of forty-six interviews with RCIA coordinators in suburban and city parishes. We wanted to obtain a broad picture of whether or not the RCIA was a reality in parishes generally as well as a more specific picture of how the policies of the RCIA were being implemented in the trenches of parish life. Although we discovered the RCIA is generally implemented in some fashion in most parishes of the archdiocese, the specific implementation of the RCIA varies greatly.

The first step was to mail a survey to the parishes of the Archdiocese in order to gather basic sociodemographic data on RCIA coordinators, what the coordinators considered to be the most serious issues related to the RCIA, and what aspects of the RCIA were actually being implemented in their parishes. The survey was mailed to 315 parishes with 282 parishes responding, a response rate of 89.5 percent. Table 6.1 below provides data on the number and percentage of RCIA coordinators. The two basic categories of RCIA coordinators are laity (non-ordained) and religious (nuns/sisters, brothers, and ordained deacons and priests). Interestingly, Table 6.1 shows that 57.5 percent of RCIA coordinators are women and 41.5 percent are men.

Table 6.1: RCIA Coordinators in the Archdiocese of Detroit

RCIA Coordinators	Number	Percentage
Laywomen	103	36.5
Priests	72	25.5
Religious Women	59	20.8
Laymen	33	11.7
Deacons	10	3.5
Unknown	3	1.0
Religious Men	2	1.0
Totals	282	100.0

Source: Archdiocese of Detroit, 1991

Overall, that is a more balanced percentage than first imagined because it is well known, based on a number of data sources[9], that women outnumber men in ministerial positions three to one except in those statuses where women are excluded (priests and deacons). Eliminating from the men all those who are priests, however, produces a closer correspondence to national data figures, with 57.5 percent being lay or religious women and 12.7 percent lay or religious men. Once again, in this rather new ministry in the church, women represent a substantial presence in parishes of the Archdiocese.

Secondly, we conducted forty-six one-and-a-half hour taped interviews with RCIA coordinators in the Detroit Archdiocese. We drew a purposive sampling when we noticed the importance of geographic location of parishes, whether they are in cities or suburbs. Suburban coordinators, we discovered, were white, whereas city coordinators were white, black and brown. These differences did not merely reflect ecological location; they also pertained to implementation strategies of the RCIA. All suburban coordinators were white whereas city coordinators were 23.5 percent black, 33 percent Hispanic, and 43.5 percent white. So there is a greater racial mix among city coordinators than suburban coordinators. But not only are suburban coordinators homogeneous in terms of race, they are also much more homogeneous than city coordinators in terms of their participation in the liturgical social network of the archdiocese, as will be described shortly.

We found that city coordinators were less likely to have a liturgical background and consequently were less connected to the liturgical social networks.

Table 6.2 shows the relationship between parish location and liturgical background of RCIA coordinators and where they received their liturgical training.

Table 6.2: Percentage Distributions of Liturgical Backgrounds of RCIA Coordinators

Parish Location	Liturgy Degree	FORUM* Workshops	Notre Dame Workshops	LTP* Workshops	Archdiocese Workshops	IPLM*
Suburbs	7 (28%)	25 (100%)	25 (100%)	25 (100%)	25 (100%)	25 (100%)
City	1 (4.7%)	3 (14.2%)	1 (4.7%)	2 (9.5%)	18 (85.7%)	6 (28.5%)

Source: Archdiocese of Detroit, 1995

*FORUM—North American Forum on the Catechumenate
*LTP—Liturgy Training Publications
*IPLM—Institute for Pastoral Liturgical Ministers (involved attending undergraduate courses)

The table clearly shows that suburban coordinators have extensive training and education in liturgy compared to city coordinators who have very little. Liturgical training is a key social organizational factor. The differences we found between suburban and city coordinators were greatly influenced by whether or not a coordinator had been trained in liturgy, as we will discover in the next chapter as well. Moreover, the differences found among suburban coordinators were due to the extent of liturgical training, that is, those coordinators with extensive training were more rigid about implementing all of the policies of the RCIA than those with less extensive training. Also, the differences found among city coordinators were due to the extent of liturgical training as well. City coordinators with more liturgical training adapted or altered the RCIA policies less than those with no training. Indeed, this factor of liturgical training was a primary differentiating factor that influenced considerably the typology of RCIA coordinators that we discuss fully in the next section.

As we have theorized throughout, as policies flow through various and different social contexts those very same policies are often interpreted differently. As we discovered with RCIA coordinators, where they received their liturgical training is important. Liturgical training and the understanding of liturgical policies and principles became more narrowly understood as the liturgical education flows downward from Vatican II to the liturgical professors in universities who train diocesan worship directors. Then those who graduate from the university often take up positions in diocesan worship offices who then establish liturgy training workshops for parish ministers (RCIA coordinators). These parish ministers then go back to their parishes to implement these liturgical policies. The problem, as we try to explain, is that these liturgical policies, in this case RCIA policies, have been honed down by the time they are discussed at diocesan workshops and the result is often a narrow understanding of the particular liturgical policies under review than when these same principles and policies were discussed at Vatican II or the university. This narrowing of liturgical policies process greatly influences the coordinators' definition of the RCIA situation and consequently their RCIA implementation strategies.

For example, in comparing city and suburban coordinator data, several differences in overall implementation strategies surfaced. At this point we began to construct social types of coordinators based on the strategies they used in implementing the RCIA. Two coordinator strategies, RCIA text-adherers and text-adapters, became master categories for identifying the various kinds of implementation strategies. Four basic social types of coordinators emerged: 1) text-adherers or suburban coordinators who implemented the RCIA according to the ritual book (for example, they maintained the year-long process of initiation as the text recommends); 2) text-adapters, or city coordinators who did not rely on the ritual book or adapted it radically (for example, they found the year-long process an obstacle to initiation); and two other social types that steered a middle road, 3) moderate text-adherers, or suburban coordinators who adapted the rite when possible but nevertheless maintained a certain faithfulness to the ritual book (for example, they reduced the timeline for initiation down to six to nine months), and 4) moderate text-adapters, or city coordinators who had little problem adapting the ritual text quite freely and broadly but realize, nevertheless, that certain aspects of the text are worth implementing at the parish level (for example, they maintained a one to three month timeline for initiation).

About a quarter of the way through our interviews, we found that suburban coordinators implemented the RCIA more rigidly than city coordinators. When we investigated the coordinators' backgrounds further, two very interesting factors stood out. As mentioned above, suburban coordinators had strong liturgical backgrounds and, second, the social and communal context of the city differed radically from the perceived individualistic suburban context. Combining a city coordinator with little liturgical background with a strong communal context, one finds extreme deviations from the ritual book's policies in terms of the implementation of the RCIA. And combining a suburban coordinator with a strong liturgical background, along with the perception of suburbia as an individualistic context, one finds extreme embracement or adherence to the ritual book's policies as a means of implementation. Consequently, all policy adherers were suburban coordinators, and all policy adapters were city coordinators. Regardless of the social type of coordinator, however, they all expressed concerns of one sort or another about the policy concerning the timeline for initiation. Table 6.3 shows the distribution of these social types of RCIA coordinators as we turn now to a further analysis of how the liturgical policies of the RCIA were altered by each type of coordinator.

Table 6.3: RCIA Coordinator Social Types

Parish Location	Text Adherer	Text Adapter	Moderate Text Adherer	Moderate Text Adapter	Total
Suburb	15	0	10	0	25
City	0	13	0	8	21
Total	15	13	10	8	46

Source: Archdiocese of Detroit, 1995

The Problem of Time

All of the RCIA coordinators we interviewed told stories of conflicts over time; stories about not having enough time to implement the RCIA fully, time going too fast during the initiation process, and conflicting church and initiate calendars. We found a basic difference, however, between suburban and city coordinators, which we think of as the ecology of the RCIA. This difference turned on whether initiates already held contractual (rational/instrumental) or covenantal (emotional/communal) social relationships. Suburban coordinators desired that initiates establish covenantal social relations during the initiation process but dealt primarily with initiates who were already embedded in contractual social relations. In contrast, city coordinators faced initiates who were already embedded in covenantal social relations. This critical difference in our understanding of the RCIA emerged when city and suburban RCIA coordinators commented on or discussed the idea of community and the temporal policies of the RCIA.

Suburban Coordinators

As mentioned above, suburban coordinators assumed a lack of community in the suburbs, and that consequently those wishing to join the parish were devoid of community. This assumption was partially grounded in the belief that suburbia was individualistic and anomic. On the other hand, these same coordinators perceived the Catholic church as a communally-oriented institutional force capable of countering individualism. Moreover, the RCIA was deliberate about initiating persons into a communal, sacramental reality, not into cultural individualism. Given this communal void in suburbia, suburban coordinators perceived the RCIA as the means for creating community and maintaining a counter-cultural stance, demarcating a crisp Catholic identity. The RCIA would be the antidote to a pervasive individualism running rampant in suburbia generally and in their parishes particularly.[10]

Although coordinators blamed individualism for creating difficulties in implementing the RCIA, they especially blamed it for altering the temporal dimension of the RCIA and thus the very essence of the initiation process. The following comments about the RCIA's temporal policies reflect the standard position of many suburban coordinators:

> Of course the problem is with the people coming in. They are used to the school year calendar and so they come in September and we accept them but we seldom get anyone like in January or May or something. So people are geared to the secular school calendar but we are introducing them to the church, which is on a liturgical calendar not the secular calendar. And so here is a major battle between these calendars. How do you initiate them not only into the church but into the liturgical calendar's rhythms. . . . I mean many scholars working in the church have said that the number one problem we face as a church is American individualism and the calendar speaks of the communal dimension and so I bring that out. It's just that most don't get it but we keep trying.

This coordinator's interpretation of parishioners and initiates "not getting it" as an outcome of the anti-Catholic ideology of individualism serves as his rationale for adhering to the yearlong RCIA process.

Another suburban coordinator, liturgically trained, believed in getting tougher about initiation in terms of the liturgical year because individualism was causing temporal problems for her and the church.

> We have it set up so that people wishing to enter the church can come in any time but most come in September and are baptized at Easter. Now granted most of them are candidates not catechumens [candidates are those baptized in another church tradition and catechumens are those never baptized] but we even end up doing the catechumens because of the strong group process but not always. We are beginning to get much tougher about this. I really shouldn't say tougher. Not tougher but more adamant about the liturgical year process especially given the suburbs and the pervasive lack of community and the abundance of individualism.

Finally, several suburban coordinators believed the RCIA was the antidote to individualism or at least a corrective. The following suburban coordinator felt this strongly:

> Right, the group process works. You know the interaction that occurs among the members or the initiates is really what makes the RCIA work, I mean they become like a little community and you want that because the RCIA is all about community. That is, it is a communal process or I should say it ultimately is about being initiated into this community and so it is at bottom a communal ex-

perience versus a strictly individual experience. I mean you have to come to recognize Jesus in the community not just in your own individual heart although that is very important. But anyway, if the personalities I guess clique in the group it can be very powerful experience. I think sometimes that this is the first community any of them have experienced outside their families. We live in such a culture of individualism which tells us to stay busy and get ahead in the secular world that we don't have time to connect with other people to build community. I mean I have a hard time just remaining in touch with my larger family. So I think individualism has something to do with it and then they experience community and they say wow this is great and they really get to know one another and to come to care for one another.

Another suburban coordinator, believed as well in the potential of the RCIA to curb individualism and induce a sense of community:

So yea, the sharing, their getting to know one another, their sense they are becoming a community especially since many of them come from you know the suburbs where there is very little community. Indeed, most of Americans are highly individualistic and so this offers them a sense of community through the group process of sharing and lectionary based catechesis. They realize they are not alone you know.

City Coordinators

City coordinators, on the other hand, did not assume that the initiates or the parish at-large lacked a sense of community or that individualism was surreptitiously eroding church community. Indeed, in the predominantly black and Hispanic parishes initiates were really "already members" of the church community, given their ten to sometimes twenty years of participation. City initiates possessed "already membership status," in other words, but had not yet celebrated formal sacramental initiation. Consequently, most city coordinators found the RCIA to be an obstacle to ritual initiation. For example, a black coordinator illustrated this when he expressed a concern about initiates being forced through "formal initiation:"

Many of the initiates come and they have been praying all their life. A number of people were even participating at Mass, not going to communion I don't think but their children, some anyway, have gone to Catholic school, and they have gone to church for many years, and so they have been participating at Mass and many people think they are Catholic. And then something comes up and like you go over the registration card and you find out this person has never been baptized and all they need is just an invitation to come in. But then you look at the process of the RCIA that you have to form them in you know forming them in prayer and in the spirit and in the knowledge of scriptures. But then I look and the people in my class had been doing scripture study, they were acquainted with old testament, new testament, prophets, gospels, they knew the difference between them and everything, and so you just don't have to take them through that type of formal initiation. Because people have been acquainted with it. The prayer "Our Father" they all knew even the unbaptized ones. So you know.

This coordinator refused to impose on these initiates a yearlong process of initiation with ongoing scriptural or lectionary-based catechesis when they were "already members" in every conceivable way but institutionally. Their sense of belonging legitimized his allowing them to circumvent extensive initiatory ritualization.

Another city coordinator, a woman, spoke more directly to the predicament she found herself in because of "already membership status:"

My experience in this city parish, actually situated in a neighborhood that is all African-American, is that the people coming in are from the neighborhood. Also, they all come out of Christian traditions, you know. Mostly Baptist, one is the church of Christ. So as I gather together with them it is a whole different experience. . . . They are people coming to the church for some reason, usually because of someone in the neighborhood. And this year more than ever, 5 or 6 people because of that. And so because of their Christian background they come with a very rich tradition of scripture and so we do a different process than the RCIA of sorts. . . . So because of their strong Christian background I hesitantly approach them to ask them to receive the sacraments officially. It was out of sorts because they had already become members in a way and so now to ask them to do these rituals was strange kind of. So we decided not to wait till the Easter Vigil and just initiate them now at the upcoming Sunday Mass. Because their readiness to me was already there. And then there were several others too who were in the same boat you know, that is who were very active in the church before going through the RCIA. And so it is odd. I mean some of them are already receiving communion and everything.

This coordinator referred twice to the oddness of her situation because of the institutional demands of the church regarding the practice of initiation. Nevertheless, she decided to bypass the church's requirement of going through a lengthy process of initiation and decided instead to "officially" initiate them immediately. Later in the interview she seemed to be at greater ease about her predicament:

You just learn to take what you need from the RCIA and if you just need to do the sacraments you just do the sacraments and in some other cases you can do a lengthier thing but even then it has been not too long because of their backgrounds, their rich scriptural and Christian backgrounds. And this I just had to learn and let go of stuff about the RCIA in the book.

Clearly this coordinator saw the RCIA presented in the institutional book as an obstacle to ritual initiation. Her definition of the situation as coordinator evolved over time and no doubt filled with personal and pastoral struggles. But in the end, she pastorally gave priority to the people over the ritual, a priority suburban coordinators had greater difficulty acknowledging.

Another city coordinator was direct about not following the RCIA because of the already membership status because it causes a "sticky situation:"

> I am suppose to tell you I am doing everything by the book, doing everything right but I am not going to lie. They are initiated at the Easter Vigil but you have to realize a lot of these people have been coming to this parish for years but that doesn't necessarily mean they are officially Catholic. But they already feel that they are a part of it. So therefore you don't want to break the, you don't want to separate them with classes or rituals because it is a sticky situation sometimes and so you don't want to make that separation because they have already been coming here. And it might be that someone will say to me you know that this person has never been initiated in the church or whatever and then I might have a discussion with them and they'll come forward. But they feel you know as if they are a part of it [parish community]. So it is just a matter of doing something official and often that is all we do. You know my Dad went to a Catholic church for as long as I can remember, I'm a cradle Catholic, but my father wasn't, yet he went to church every Sunday, he only got baptized when he was in his sixties (laughing). But he felt he was part of the parish and, I guess it was something that was done to him when he entered a church in California—he stopped going—and then until he came back here you know he was then baptized because they made him feel that he wasn't part of that California church. And so I guess I am very sensitive and conscious of that fact and so I try to understand that and so I often overlook much of the RCIA.

Clearly, he situates his ministerial priorities with the people and not with church RCIA policies.

Common to all of these RCIA coordinators as they confronted the situation of "already membership status" was their granting priority to the people over the ritual. In their pastoral judgment, belonging to the community outweighed any ritual requirements even though they respected those requirements. Indeed, they still wanted people to be sacramentally initiated, but they perceived the many preparation rituals as well as the catechetical and scriptural requirements as obstacles to initiation and therefore adapted or simply dropped them. Nevertheless, all of the coordinators struggled with this "already membership status" on the one hand and the RCIA's ritual requirements on the other hand. In the end, however, their coaching methods gave honor to the people and the people's sense of social solidarity while simultaneously diminishing the emphasis on the ritual requirements of the RCIA.

Negotiation and Rationality

In turning our attention to how coordinators dealt with the prescriptive RCIA temporal order, we observe that most of them organized the liturgical year according to contractual, secular social relations. For example, many coordinators allowed initiates to negotiate the time it takes to complete the RCIA process rather than make them commit to the church's sequencing. Often this led to a mutual agreement to truncate the process of initiation to five or seven months in suburban parishes and often much less time in city parishes. Negotiation is a central component of contractual social relations, and as Bromley and Busching[11] point out, negotiation rather than bonding reflects a more contractual expectation of social relations. For example, one suburban coordinator noted:

> After talking with most inquirers (those seeking entrance into the church), I found that they are simply too busy. And it's a joke to think that we could get them to attend during summer months.

Another suburban coordinator said:

> Many of those wanting to become Catholic told me that they had children and that it wouldn't be possible to attend all of the sessions. It was after hearing this time and again that I shortened the RCIA and realized it would be better to initiate adults according to their children's calendar. So if you ask me, what the school demands is more important than what the church wants.

One suburban coordinator apologized for the timeline after seeing the shocked look on initiates' faces—a non-verbal means of negotiation. Another coordinator understood the import of the liturgical year but found that many of the college student initiates were locked into other calendars.

> We might have a few pre-evangelization sessions, you know, a couple of sharing sessions with the group and then subsequent to that the regular formal sessions begin in mid-October and continue throughout until Easter time. And we don't go after Easter time, no no, I wouldn't say. You know there are a lot of young people involved and they have their things to do, for example, their classes, not so much their classes but their times for study and so forth and there are conflicts here and there but they are fairly good about advising us of those occasions when they come up and fairly faithful I would say in their attendance. But year round no.

Yet another suburban coordinator believed in the liturgical year as well but through pastoral practice discovered it did not work. As she expressed it, people are just too busy today:

Making it more than one year is hard. I think you do well getting them in August and September and preparing them for the Easter, the coming Easter Vigil. We had in all the years that I have been doing it, we have had a couple of people who stayed over for more than one year. But that is a rarity. People today have extremely busy lives and if you tell them going in—I mean if you tell them going in that its going to be nine to twelve months they look at you like "you've got to be kidding." Now ideally I agree whole heartily with the premise that it should take a longer time.

This coordinator still believed in the liturgical year and the lengthier process of initiation but she adjusted to the situation of peoples' lives and adapted the rite.

Another suburban coordinator based her pastoral adjustments on the needs of the group:

The liturgical year, the full thing, depends on the group again. Usually with all the groups we go through till Pentecost and then depending on the group I will continue if it is their desire. I have some groups that, you know, say "hey I need some time off. But there are other groups who say no this is fine and we would like to come back again. So the invitation is always open.

Overall, the coordinator framed the RCIA process in the liturgical year but did not insist on it. She accommodated her groups whether they wanted a summer break or not. Her comments illustrate the attempt to maintain a liturgical year framework and at the same time remain flexible. She went on to say:

Once again, it depends on your group whether or not more or less time is needed with them. The dynamics of every group is so different. It is mind boggling. I have notes from year to year and I say wow this worked great last year and so I will use this again this year and then find that this doesn't suit the dynamics of that particular group. So you have to change.

With that statement, she gave priority to the people over the text but not to the extent that city coordinators did. The next coordinator also was confident in not following the year-round approach because it was not practical for initiates:

Well, the calendar. September through May is our process. And even after reading commentaries and reflections by people who steer away from that and promote the liturgical year, year round approach, from a practical point of view people's lives revolve around one, their school—when their kids are in school—and most people take time off during the Summer to play. And I think people in the church need to do that to and so that is my response to all those commentaries.

Although strict about implementing certain aspects of the RCIA, such as lectionary-based catechesis, she was willing to adapt to people's secular calendars. A city coordinator, in contrast, summed up the city perspective this way:

> I think that, because of the culture of the people and their 'already' kind of be-
> longing, that for them to say 'I've got to wait that long' we have to take seri-
> ously. I mean really, that is a long time to them, especially since they feel they
> already belong. A year process is an obstacle here. So we don't do it.

As a result of people already belonging to the community (city initiates), being
too busy, adhering to school calendars, or experiencing initial shock at the
length of time required (suburban initiates), coordinators adjusted to and accommodated the initiates' social situation, resulting in a temporal patterning of
initiation different from the church's mandated policy.

There were some suburban coordinators, more liturgically trained, however,
who did not change the church's stance on the one-year minimum timeline after
negotiating with initiates. For example, a coordinator in a middle class, white,
suburban parish reported:

> In talking with inquirers I don't apologize for what the RCIA is or the length of
> time it requires. I believe in it and I think it is just fine. People will follow what
> the church asks if you stick to your guns. If I begin apologizing the people will
> think it is unjust. So I go with it.

Another coordinator in an upper-class suburban neighborhood said:

> We abide by the yearlong catechumenate. Once, a couple living together com-
> plained about this cutting into their work time. At that point we challenged
> them about their priorities by asking them about their standard of living and
> that maybe they needed to reconsider that standard.

Although these coordinators followed the church's mandate, their stories still
reveal problems that center on the issue of time. But they used their understanding of the RCIA to uphold rather than change the time-order of initiation set
down by the church policies.

Rationality is a major interaction component in contractual social relations.
Specifically, relationships dominated by rationality entail the priorities of self-
interest, logic, calculation, and reason. In covenantal social relations, however,
people express and convey connection, involvement, and identification with one
another.[12] So in contractual relations employers and employees routinely negotiate work schedules, task responsibilities, performance, and money. Conversely,
in covenantal social relations the covenant is communicated through language of
commitment, tradition, and enduring bonds.

As already noted, suburban RCIA coordinators shortened the initiation
process to accommodate initiates' time constraints, sequenced initiation according to the school calendar to accommodate initiates' children, and sometimes
apologized for the length of time required and then proceeded to shorten it. City

coordinators, on the other hand, often bypassed the entire initiation process. Initiates rationally negotiated their timetables according to their self-interest. And coordinators rationally negotiated a time frame more in accord with the secular time frame of the initiates. Even suburban coordinators who did not change the yearlong timeline still had to rationally negotiate for their position. City coordinators, however, faced with people who were "already members" disregarded the RCIA because initiations into covenantal social relations were already established. Only the formal, public ritual needed to be enacted for these initiates. In the city parish, where covenantal bonds are already evident, coordinators deemed it "rational" to conclude that a lengthy initiation process was unnecessary.

The initiates themselves often rationally negotiated with RCIA coordinators about the temporal ordering of initiation. As one suburban coordinator said, "Most people want to know what is required, and then after I tell them they want to know if there is a quicker way." Another suburban coordinator logically and rationally concluded that having "fifteen minute zinger sessions" was the best way to implement the RCIA. As she noted: "I realize that initiates' schedules are chuck full, especially if they are parents, so I try to at least zap them with something—so I have fifteen minute zinger sessions."

Another way inquirers rationally negotiate is by asking about other parishes where they might pursue the RCIA because the time at their parishes do not meet their needs. Some coordinators were upset by this. For example, one suburban coordinator commented:

> I understand that people don't have a lot of time, but we are talking about being initiated into the church, into faith, and into faith in a local community, not the amorphous reality of the universal Catholic church. So when people come to me from another parish to attend our sessions because it is more convenient for them and their schedules, I just get frustrated, even annoyed. I mean initiation is about entering this community and forming relationships in the community where you will be baptized and so not to be involved with that community from the beginning really makes no theological sense. So I tell them no. I have though for people in this parish, changed the timeframe so they could get baptized in this church, you know like having sessions at another time and in some cases having a much shorter timeline.

Here again is someone rationally negotiating different avenues to becoming Catholic besides the one afforded by his parish. The interview went on to reveal that the candidate actually hoped that this coordinator's RCIA was not as lengthy as that at his parish or have as many requirements. A similar situation occurred with the following suburban coordinator:

> Honestly, I couldn't believe the nerve of this woman. She simply pranced in and wanted to know how long our RCIA program was and what were the requirements. And before I could answer her, she went on in a very derogatory

tone about her parish and the unrealistic expectations of the person in charge of the program there. She just wanted it her way, never giving what the church might expect a moment's thought. It just makes you mad.

These last few quotes reveal how candidates can give little credence to the institutional church and want an initiation process that fits their needs. Sociologists of religion have noted again and again the shift in the locus of religious authority from the institution to the individual. It appears to be no different in matters of initiation.

Conclusion

Problems of time can be lodged in a number of processes, but the problematics of time for the RCIA coordinators we studied rested in the tensions between the church's prescriptive policy of a sacred temporal order versus various secular temporal orders. From the point of view of the church, the establishment of covenantal relations and the full absorption of persons into the spiritual community of Catholics was at issue. To accomplish the church's policies and goals, the RCIA, constituted of various steps and a one-year time frame, was to guide coordinators' activities as they sought to move persons through the status passage process. The only aspect of this process that was consistent across all cases in our data appears to be the desire for and focus on the end product of baptism during the Easter Vigil. That is the point at which candidates become "Catholics." How coordinators accomplished that desired end point, though, varied a great deal in response to local contingencies.

City coordinators were very likely to feel that a covenant already existed with their RCIA candidates because of their "already membership status." Many of them had been parishioners for years and for all practical purposes were practicing Catholics. These coordinators, therefore, quite willingly reinterpreted and shortened the RCIA's yearlong policy to only a few months. Moreover, because few of these coordinators had formal liturgical training, they felt it appropriate to adapt the prescriptive texts to the level of theological knowledge of the candidates before them. This adaptation coupled with the "already membership status" legitimized for coordinators altering the mandated RCIA policies.

Suburban coordinators seemed to struggle if not suffer more than did the city coordinators as they adapted and altered the policies of the RCIA. They usually had liturgical training and believed that the new liturgical texts were indispensable for covenantal relations. Accordingly, they tended to adhere to strict and full interpretations of the policies of the RCIA and to insist on full educational experiences for the RCIA candidates. This factor in itself extended the time frame beyond that typically found in city parishes. Suburban candidates, furthermore, came to the RCIA as nonmembers, which confirmed in their coordinators' views the candidates' individualistic attitudes and noncommunal lifestyles. Yet the challenges of school schedules, weekend activities, work demands, and social calendars that candidates brought to the RCIA induced coordinators to negotiate reduced time commitments other than the church's policy. In the process, the suburban coordinators ironically became the ones less convinced that the covenant was really present at baptism even though they more fully implemented the prescriptive temporal order policy of the RCIA.

Kavanagh[13] argues that RCIA coordinators, more than other ministers in the church, are constantly patrolling the borders of Catholic identity. They appear to have a heightened awareness of identity issues because they are constantly being confronted with what a "Catholic" is and whether RCIA candidates are becoming one. Patrolling these borders (maintaining the policies of the church) is a catch-22 situation. If coordinators let people into the church too easily (not follow the church's policies) are they compromising Catholic identity? If they are too demanding and candidates quit the RCIA, are they being inhospitable and unwelcoming? So these coordinators live in a fragile world of opening and closing the borders of the church, at the heart of which are the adjustments to the RCIA's policy regarding initiation's sacred temporal order.

Notes

1. Aidan Kavanagh, "Christian Initiation: Tactics and Strategy," in *Made, Not Born: New Perspectives on Christian Initiation and the Catechumenate*, ed. The Murphy Center for Liturgical Research (Notre Dame: University of Notre Dame Press, 1974).

2. Mark Searle, *Christening: The Making of Christians* (Collegeville: The Liturgical Press, 1980), 11.

3. Searle, *Christening* (1980).

4. Austin Flannery, ed. *Vatican II: The Conciliar and post Conciliar Documents*. (New York: Costello, 1987), 21.

5. *Rite of Christian Initiation of Adults* (Chicago: Liturgy Training Publications, 1988).

6. *Rite of Christian Initiation of Adults*, National Statutes, #6: 367.

7. David Bromley and Bruce Busching, "Understanding the Structure of Contractual and Covenantal Social Relations: Implications for the Sociology of Religion." *Sociological Analysis* 49(1988):15-32.

8. Richard Travisano, "Alternation and Conversion as Qualitatively Different Transformations." Pp. 594-606 in *Social Psychology Through Symbolic Interaction*, edited by Gregory Stone and Harvey Farberman (Toronto: Xerox College Publishing, 1970).

9. David C. Leege, "Parish Life Among the Leaders," in *Notre Dame Study of Catholic Parish Life*, Report No. 9. (Notre Dame, IN.: Institute for Pastoral and Social Ministry, 1986); Phillip Murnion and David DeLambo, *Parishes and Parish Ministries: A Study of Parish Lay Ministry* (New York: National Pastoral Life Center, 1999); and David DeLambo, *Lay Parish Ministers: A Study of Emerging Leadership* (New York: The National Pastoral Life Center, 2005).

10. Although there is a sociological literature that supports the suburban coordinator's perception of rampant individualism in suburbia, there is another body of literature that indicates the opposite. Bennett Berger, *Working Class Suburbs* (Berkeley: University of California Press, 1960); Herbert Gans, *The Urban Villagers* (New York: The Free Press, 1962); Andrew Greeley, "Habits of the Head." *Society* (May/June, 1992); Stephen Warner, "Work in Progress: Toward a New Paradigm for the Sociological Study of Religion in the United States." *American Journal of Sociology*, 98(1993): 1044-93; and Donald Capps and Richard Fenn, eds., *Individualism Reconsidered: Readings Bearing on the Endangered Self in Modern Society* (Center for Religion, Self, and Society, Princeton Theological Seminary, Monograph Series, # 1, New Jersey: A & A Printing Co., Inc), all have written about "individualism" more positively in that it does not preclude community.

11. David Bromley and Bruce Busching, "Understanding the Structure of Contractual and Covenantal Social Relations: Implications for the Sociology of Religion." *Sociological Analysis* 49S (1988): 15-32.

12. Bromley and Busching, "Understanding," 15-32.

13. Kavanagh, Aidan, "Catechesis: Formation in Stages," in *The Baptismal Mystery and the Catechumenate*, ed. Michael W. Merriman (New York: The Church Hymnal Corporation, 1990).

Chapter 7
The Tabernacle

This chapter focuses on the tabernacle (a sacred box) and Vatican II policies regulating its location, specifically whether it is to reside in the center of the church sanctuary, at the side of the church sanctuary, or outside of the church sanctuary altogether. Consistent with data pertaining to other liturgical controversies discussed throughout this book, professional liturgists and ordinary Catholic pew-dwellers differed in their views on the location of the tabernacle. Professional liturgists advocate removing the tabernacle from the main body of the church to a separate smaller space called a eucharistic chapel, while ordinary lay parishioners tend to want to be able to see and pray before the tabernacle and therefore want it to remain front and center in the main body of the church. Once again, it appears that an attitudinal and behavioral gap exists between professional ministers and ordinary pew-dwellers.

Tabernacle Location as a Problem

The tabernacle is a decorated box that often has been located behind the altar or on the main altar in the center of the church's sanctuary. In the first centuries of the church there were no tabernacles. If someone could not attend eucharist during this time, the minister would simply take consecrated bread and distribute it later to the sick, dying or those absent from Mass. Justin Martyr (ca. 150), for example, knew of the custom of taking communion (consecrated bread) to those prevented from attending the liturgy, and Hippolytus (ca. 250) spoke to the issue of Christians taking it home for communion on weekdays. There were pronouncements, however, warning Christians to keep the sacred bread in a place where rodents could not eat it.

Once Christians began building churches, the leftover sacred bread was kept in cupboards in the sacristy, the room where ministers would dress and prepare for Mass. Eventually a box-like tabernacle came into use which was located in or near the church building. Sometimes the box was "kept in the sacristy, in containers built or suspended in the main body of the church near the altar (eucharistic towers, pyxes in the shape of doves), in niches constructed in the church wall (ambries), or, increasingly after the sixteenth and seventeenth centuries, in tabernacles placed directly on the principal altar."[1]

Placing tabernacles on the principal altar continued until the advent of the Second Vatican Council. Although there were earlier discussions about the role and placement of the tabernacle, it was Vatican II that stated the theologically problematic nature of the location of the tabernacle on the principal altar. The policies adopted, however, were rather ambiguous, because there were conflicting statements about its location. Some documents stated it should be placed in a prominent location in the main church and others stated that it should be located in its own chapel separate from the main church.[2] Consequently, much confusion and controversy has resulted.

The problem addressed by Vatican II was the contention that the tabernacle overwhelmed the celebration of the eucharist. As Vatican II progressed, a eucharistic theology unfolded that emphasized the eucharist as an action; an action of God and an action of the People of God. What most bishops concluded at this time, based on much of the research done by liturgists before the council, was that the people were passive spectators in the Mass, especially in the medieval period and after, and that this situation should change so that the people become active participants in the Mass and, indeed, in all of the sacraments. The tabernacle had suddenly come to visually overwhelm the action of the eucharist and thereby contributed, so the argument went, to the inactive, unconscious, and empty participation of the faithful at Mass. Based, therefore, on the principle of the full, active, conscious participation of the faithful, the central principal of the document on the Liturgy, the tabernacle location needed to be rethought. Indeed, some documents claimed that the tabernacle should be removed from the principal altar altogether and placed in its own chapel apart from the church so that people could concentrate and participate more fully in the immediate eucharistic celebration taking place in their midst. Moreover, the earliest traditional function of the tabernacle was that of reserving the bread consecrated at Mass for those who could not attend Mass, that is, the sick. In other words, the tabernacle did not have any function at Mass other than reserving the consecrated bread for the sick, which could be done after Mass.

So the solution to the problem of the passive, spectator-like role the people played during Mass was to incorporate new policies that would increase the participation of the faithful. The purpose of the policy approach was to position the faithful as more spiritually connected to their God. The way to increase the divinization process among the people and thereby connect them more to their

God was to increase their active participation in the liturgy, and the answer was to rewrite the rules in order for that connection to occur. That is, the solution was to create rules that would help the people concentrate on the presence of God in themselves and in one another, "not in some box".

With the theology of eucharist as action in place, the Constitution on the Sacred Liturgy set the stage for further policies to be articulated that would transform sacred space in accordance with the principle of the active participation of the faithful. We therefore find statements like the following in some of the post-conciliar liturgical documents: "It is therefore recommended that, as far as possible, the tabernacle be placed in a chapel distinct from the middle or central part of the church, above all in those churches where marriages and funerals take place frequently, and in places which are much visited for their artistic or historical treasures."[3] A long explanation is given in the document *Environment and Art in Catholic Worship*[4], an American Bishops' document:

> The celebration of the eucharist is the focus of the normal Sunday assembly. As such, the major space of church is designed for this *action*. Beyond the celebration of the eucharist, the church has had a most ancient tradition of reserving the eucharistic bread. The purpose of [the] this reservation is to bring communion to the sick and to be the object of private devotion. Most appropriately, this reservation should be designated in a space designed for individual devotion. A room or chapel specifically designed and separate from the major space is important so that no confusion can take place between the celebration of the eucharist and reservation. Active and static aspects of the same reality cannot claim the same human attention at the same time.

On the other hand, documents have been promulgated that state the opposite of what was stated above. For example, in a post-conciliar document on the liturgy we read: "The Blessed Sacrament should be reserved in a solid, inviolable tabernacle in the middle of the altar or on a side altar, but in a truly prominent place."[5] In the *Code of Canon Law* we read that the Blessed Sacrament is to be reserved "in a distinguished place in a church or oratory, a place which is conspicuous, suitably adorned and conducive to prayer."[6] It goes on to say that this place is to be "very prominent, truly noble and duly decorated," implying that this should be the case whether it is located at the center of the sanctuary of the church or in a Blessed Sacrament chapel apart from the main church. Moreover, the fundamental text of the Mass states: "It is highly recommended that the holy eucharist be reserved in a chapel suitable for private adoration and prayer. If this is impossible because of the structure of the church or local custom, it should be kept on an altar or other place in the church that is prominent and properly decorated."[7] It is these conflicting policies that caught our attention and motivated us to investigate further.

Data and Methods

Our theory of policy implementation directs attention to the network of offices, organizations, and local contexts that represent the situations of implementation processes. In keeping with the methodological requirements of that theory, we have used a modified triangulated approach to data gathering and analysis, and have included as data sources the key situations and actors in the church's attempts to implement Vatican II principles of worship. The kinds of data for these sources on tabernacle location are summarized in Table 7.1.

Table 7.1: Sources and Type of Data

How Data Collected	Content	Type of Data
Parish Site Visits	Tabernacle Location	Quantitative
Phone Interviews	Tabernacle Location	Quantitative
Phone Interviews	ARC Committee	Quantitative
Personal Interview	Professional Liturgists	Qualitative
Personal Interview	Lay Parishioners	Qualitative
AOD Data Base	Location of Parishes	Quantitative

First, as articulated in the previous section, we use the actual Vatican II texts that state church policy regarding the tabernacle location. These texts, of course, are a necessary starting point for the analysis of policy processes for all of our chapters reporting on parish-level studies of liturgical implementation. This chapter as well as the previous two, therefore, adopts the sociological view that the importance of texts rests in how they are collectively acted toward. Our methodological focus then is on actors' interpretations of the textual material and the consequences of those interpretations.

Second, we have conducted studies of tabernacle location implementation processes at various levels in the Archdiocese of Detroit. We have collected participant observation data on meetings at the Archdiocesan level (Architectural Review Committee meetings of the Office of Worship) that addressed issues of tabernacle location, and we surveyed all of the parishes of the Archdiocese to determine tabernacle location. We also conducted telephone interviews with forty-three parish officials about having parish level architectural review committees as part of the parish's worship commission and we conducted short interviews with parish officials who have removed the tabernacle from the center of the church as to why they moved it and, then, subsequent interviews with laity from those same parishes about their reactions to the tabernacle's removal. We also used the Archdiocesan database to organize parishes according to geographic location (urban, suburban, and rural) for purposes of comparison. Hence, we acquired information on the history of parish tabernacle locations, if and when they were moved and where, the decision makers, the degree of difficulty in the process, parish members' participation and reactions to the moves, and the role of liturgists and Archdiocesan administrative offices in these policy implementation processes.

Data were gathered on tabernacle location in all parishes of the Archdiocese of Detroit, and these data are presented in table 7.2 below, which shows whether tabernacles are located inside or outside the sanctuary in the parishes of the Archdiocese as well as the geographic location of the parishes themselves – whether they are city, suburban, or rural parishes.

Table 7.2: Location of Tabernacle in Parishes by Geographic Location

Location	City	Suburb	Rural	Total
In Sanctuary	68 (80%)	91 (43.5%)	11 (57.9%)	170 (54.3%)
Out Sanctuary	17 (20%)	118 (56.5%)	8 (42.1%)	143 (45.7%)
Total Parishes	85 (100%)	209 (100%)	19 (100%)	313 (100%)

Source: Archdiocese of Detroit, Department of Parish Life and Services, Office of Pastoral Research, 2001.

Table 7.2 shows, overall, that there are slightly more parishes with their tabernacle located in the sanctuary rather than out of it (54.3 percent vs. 45.7 percent). However, the distribution of tabernacle location appears to be a function of parish location. That is, 80 percent of the city parishes compared to only 43.5 percent of suburban parishes locate their tabernacles inside the sanctuary, and proportionately over twice as many suburban as city parishes locate their tabernacles outside the sanctuary. Although rural parishes fall between city and suburban parishes, in that 57.9 percent locate their tabernacles in the sanctuary, they are more similar to city than suburban parishes.

Why did 80 percent of the city parishes, however, locate their tabernacles inside the sanctuary while only 43.5 percent of suburban parishes did so? Although city parishes on average have existed for more years than most suburban parishes, which is a plausible partial explanation for this difference, we believe, given our previous research, that it had more to do with the degree of liturgical presence. We contacted 43 parishes by phone to collect data on "liturgical presence" in terms of their worship commissions and art and environment (A&E)

committees. We asked several questions pertaining to how many members were
professionally trained in liturgy, whether the A&E committee had been educated
on the Vatican II documents pertaining to church architecture, whether or not
they had moved the tabernacle from the sanctuary, and whether or not there
were problems with moving the tabernacle if it had been moved. We contacted
parishes making sure that our sample included suburban and city parishes. Rural
parishes still need to be studied.

First, we wanted to know whether high or low liturgical presence was related to tabernacle location decisions and table 7.3 shows that there is such an
association. Our construct of "liturgical presence" is defined in terms of the pro-
portion of members of parish worship commissions who are professionally
trained liturgists. If 20 percent or more of these members were liturgically
trained, we coded them as having high presence; if 10 percent or less, we coded
them as having low presence.

Table 7.3: Liturgical Presence and Tabernacle Location Decisions

Liturgical Presence	Tabernacle Moved	Tabernacle Not Moved
High	21 (72%)	8 (28%)
Low	4 (29%)	10 (71%)

Source: Archdiocese of Detroit, Department of Parish Life and Services, Office of Pastoral Research, 2001.

Parishes with high liturgical presence, we found, are more likely to move their
tabernacle (72 percent) and parishes with low liturgical presence are more likely
to leave them in their original locations (71 percent). As to whether or not high
liturgical presence was associated with problems concerning the moving of the
tabernacle, table 7.4 shows there is. Parishes with high liturgical presence are
more likely to encounter problems, whether they move their tabernacles or not
(83 percent), whereas none of the parishes with low liturgical presence reported
major problems.

Table 7.4: Liturgical Presence and Problems in Moving Tabernacle

Liturgical Presence	High/Moderate Problems	Not a Problem
High	24 (83%)	5 (17%)
Low	0	14 (100%)

Source: Archdiocese of Detroit, Department of Parish Life and Services, Office of Pastoral Research, 2001.

When we factored in geographic location and whether or not there was a problem or not in moving the tabernacle, we found that city parishes that move their tabernacles are somewhat more likely to encounter problems than suburban parishes that do so (90 percent vs. 67 percent—see table 7.5), although both tend to have problems.

Table 7.5: Whether Moving the Tabernacle Was a Problem

Moved Tabernacle	City Parishes	Suburban Parishes
Problem	9 (90%)	10 (67%)
Not a problem	1	5
Subtotals	10	15

Did Not Move Tabernacles	City Parishes	Suburban Parishes
Problem	2 (20%)	3 (38%)
Not a problem	8	5
Subtotals	10	8

Source: Archdiocese of Detroit, Department of Parish Life and Services, Office of Pastoral Research, 2001.

Suburban parishes that leave the tabernacle in its original location are about twice as likely to have problems as are city parishes that do so (38 percent vs. 20 percent). The reason, again, is partly due to high or low liturgical presence. When dealing with the issue of tabernacle location, as table 7.6 shows, suburban parishes are more likely than city parishes to draw on worship commissions and professional personnel.

Table 7.6: Decision-makers in Tabernacle Location Deliberations

	City Parishes	Suburban Parishes
Architectural Review Committee	11 (55%)	17 (74%)
Director of Religious Education	0 (0%)	7 (30%)
Pastor	14 (70%)	19 (83%)
Parishioners	6 (30%)	5 (22%)
Priest	0 (0%)	2 (9%)
Worship Commission	10 (50%)	16 (70%)
Organist	10 (50%)	12 (52%)
Liturgical Consultant	8 (40%)	14 (61%)
Total Parishes	20	23

Source: Archdiocese of Detroit, Department of Parish Life and Services, Office of Pastoral Research, 2001.

Suburban parishes also are more likely to use liturgical consultants (61 percent vs. 40 percent), to have worship committee meetings (70 percent vs. 50 percent), involve priests (9 percent vs. 0 percent), or pastors (83 percent vs. 70 percent), as well as DREs (30 percent vs. 0 percent), and ARC (74 percent vs. 55 percent). And table 7.7 shows that whenever these ranges of resources are used, they tend to result in or become involved in major problems in the parish deliberation process.

Table 7.7: Magnitude of Problem Moving Tabernacle

	High	% Liturgists	Low		N=
Architectural Review Committee	23 (82%)		5		28
Director of Religious Education	6 (86%)		1		7
Pastor	24 (73%)	(79%)	9	(77%)	33
Parishioners	10 (91%)		1		11
Priest	2 (100%)	(100%)	0		2
Pastoral Minister	4 (100%)		0		4
Worship Commission	21 (81%)		5		26
Organist	18 (82%)	(78%)	4	(25%)	22
Liturgical Consultant	19 (86%)		3		22

Source: Archdiocese of Detroit, Department of Parish Life and Services, Office of Pastoral Research, 2001.

In sum, when parishes go through the process of moving their tabernacles, they tend to have major problems (84 percent), strong opposition (64 percent), and strong liturgical influence (76 percent). When parishes leave their tabernacles in their original location, they tend to have minor or no problems at all (72 percent), medium to very low levels of opposition (61 percent), and weak to moderate liturgical influence (83 percent). Levels of difficulty (86 percent), strong opposition (64 percent), and strong liturgical influence (82 percent) tend to be higher when parishes have moved their tabernacle two or more times.

Laity and Liturgists

Realizing there were problems and tensions with moving the tabernacle, we wanted to know who had the problem and why. Consequently, we selected parishes that had been involved in church renovation and had contacted the Architectural Review Committee of the Archdiocese. The majority of these parishes were suburban (95 percent), white, and middle class. Consequently, generalizations to the entire Archdiocese are not made, although we suspect the findings would be generalizable to suburban parishes. Moreover, further specification of the variety of types of laity and types of liturgists would be needed as well. The laity, for example, is a very broad category of the Catholic faithful who vary in their beliefs, attitudes, and behavior. We suspect that laity who volunteer to sit on parish level A&E committees, for example, are of different liturgical persuasions, some representing the ordinary Catholic in the pew and others more aligned with professional liturgists who have taught lay A&E members about the liturgy of the church. In other words, we believe that the laity who sit on various types of commissions and committees at the parish level may well represent a midgroup between pew-dwelling laity and lay professional ministers. The thirty parishes that became part of this research represent 9.6 percent of the parishes of the Detroit Archdiocese. We conducted forty short interviews, twenty-five with lay people and fifteen with professionals. Usually, after a parish committee meeting or an ARC meeting we would approach staff professionals or lay members and ask them if we could interview them about tabernacle location. If they said yes, which all of them did, then we would proceed to ask them the following questions: 1) Where would you like to see the tabernacle located in your church? 2) Why do you want it located there? Considerable divergence in interpretation of liturgical principles emerged between ordinary laity and church professionals.

Laity Views

One group of laity, for example, simply wanted to "see" the tabernacle. Although their explanations tended to be theologically unsophisticated, they not only believed them to be important, but they felt strongly about the issue. For example, one woman said, "I can't believe they moved the tabernacle to this back room that used to be the cry room. Now I cannot see the tabernacle at all from the main body of the church. Why can't I see it?" A young man told us, "In our church the tabernacle has been put over on the side. It's not even central, you can hardly see it. So now even when I go pray it feels different to me, like it's not as important." Another woman just blurted out, "By putting the tabernacle on the side of the church it's saying that it's not important. Jesus is there and we're putting him in the corner."

Although the above comments are straightforward and lack any developed theology, other laity on A&E committees educated themselves about the theology and ecclesiology involved with the issue of the tabernacle and even what the liturgical documents spelled out on this issue. In the end, they were able to encounter the liturgists with their own semi-developed perspectives of the issue and on what the church had to say about the role of the tabernacle. In other words, some laity were able to argue with the liturgists' definition of the situation of removing the tabernacle as a means of enhancing the principle of active participation. These data suggest that the professionals were teaching A&E committee members about the liturgy and the various documents that apply to church renovation. In many cases, professionals won the laity over to their point of view through this educational process, but not entirely. Most of the laity we talked to were not convinced about what the professionals were suggesting regarding the location of the tabernacle and consequently decided to do some investigating of their own. Moreover, others began to understand that the driving principle behind the liturgical changes was the principle of active participation, and so they began to use that same principle to justify their own point of view— much like the laity did with the issue of seating and first holy communion discussed in chapter 5. For example, one woman on her parish's A&E committee said,

> I understand that the document "Environment and Art in Catholic Worship" recommends building a eucharistic chapel separate from the main body of the church but it doesn't demand it. Other liturgy documents, like the GIRM (General Instruction of the Roman Missal), do not require it being removed although it allows the tabernacle to be moved. Some liturgical documents talk about preserving the sacred images in the church and not moving them or dismantling them in any way because of their value. So it seems to me that we don't have to move it.

Responding to a liturgist's reference to the fundamental liturgical principle of Vatican II, that is, the full, active, and conscious participation of the faithful (the principle liturgists use to justify removing the tabernacle from the sanctuary— and to be discussed further below), a man from a suburban parish noted:

> I don't see where having the tabernacle up behind the altar on the backside of the apse is going to take away from the active participation of the people. I think it enhances their participation when they can see the tabernacle because it evokes a sense of reverence and that is a form of participation I think. So to remove everything but the altar in order for us to focus on the altar and the people around it is not the only way to enhance participation.

These few quotes from laity on A&E committees suggest a liturgical awareness beyond the average pew-dwelling parishioner's understanding about removing the tabernacle, but as ordinary parishioners themselves they still do not like the tabernacle being removed.

Finally, to show the extent of some laity's feelings about this liturgical issue, one man sent a petition to all parishioners saying that the pastor was going to renovate the church and that the tabernacle would no longer be seen. The letter goes on to quote Canon Law, number 938 that we read earlier, that the tabernacle should be in a conspicuous place in the church. The curious point here is that the pastor is not removing the tabernacle but simply enhancing the spot where it is and enclosing it in decorative housing. Indeed, he is open to having glass in the enclosure so the tabernacle can be seen. So he is trying to make it visible and at the same time is not removing it. Nevertheless, this petition was drawn up. So even when very little is being changed, people get upset that the tabernacle is being tampered with. The man who organized the petition had this to say:

> Sure, the pastor tells us that he is not doing much to the space but he is. And the next thing you know we will not be able to see it. We want to see it. The building was built to emphasize this spot where the tabernacle is and now they are going to change it and that'll mean not being able to see the tabernacle or moving it to some obscure place in the church. There isn't much left, let's at least keep the tabernacle.

This man seemed to be at his wits end. He went on to say that he didn't like what he was doing but he felt he had to make a stand. In particular, he went into detail about the church's architecture, and how the tower protruding from the center of the church was built to look like a silo because this area was known for its farming. Moreover, it had eucharistic symbolism in that farming wheat for making bread is symbolic of Jesus the bread of life. Building the silo was also a means of emphasizing where the bread of life was reserved – in the tabernacle. He therefore interpreted any tampering with the tabernacle or tabernacle area to be a change not respectful of the original intent of the church building. Given all of the interviews and discussions we heard from laypeople, the most common response to the lack of a centrally located tabernacle was, "now our church seems empty."

Professional Views

Professional liturgists, on the other hand, wanted the tabernacle removed, as we noted earlier. Just to round out the data, we hear now, in their own words, from professional liturgists who dealt with this issue. Again, their arguments are not flippant but based on ecclesiological and liturgical principles found in the Constitution on the Sacred Liturgy. For example, a liturgist at a local, suburban parish stated the following:

The people have to come to understand Vatican II. It called for a shift to assembly or congregational participation. Assembly is really the better term because that includes the priest. He is not just running the show anymore. He is
an active participant in the liturgy like everyone else. So that is the liturgical
principle we are basing our decision on to move the tabernacle. The church has
called us to focus more on the altar and the people around it rather than the tabernacle. So the tabernacle has to be removed from center stage because otherwise it obscures the focus of Sunday liturgy.

Another liturgist said:

We need to move the people to a new vision of church. I think it is really an ecclesiological issue. What does it mean to be church? It certainly isn't to worship a gold box (tabernacle). We need to find Jesus in one another and so the
focus of the liturgy is on the people not the tabernacle and that kind of emphasis flows from how we view church, our ecclesiology. The church is the people
of God. How can we accentuate that reality, not the reality of Jesus in a box?
So the tabernacle is removed and the altar with the people gathered around it
become central.

This line of argumentation flows into an understanding or theology of eucharist
as well. Liturgists argue that the tabernacle is a distraction during the liturgy,
primarily the celebration of the Mass, and therefore the areas of celebration
(eucharist) and reservation (tabernacle) must be separate. Otherwise, an undo
theological emphasis is given to the devotion of the sacrament, which detracts
from the premier presence of Christ found in the celebration of the Sunday
Mass. As one liturgist noted:

With Mother Angelica on TV I now hear from the parishioners that we should
be having more eucharistic devotions. I mean we are going back to the experience of church before Vatican II. The eucharist is a thing again rather than an
action of the people in Christ. In the medieval period we say that the eucharist
had become reified or thingified, you know the host itself. People just come to
look at it but not partake of it. This is getting bad.

Professional liturgists wanted the tabernacle removed from the center of the
sanctuary because they thought it would enhance the active participation of the
faithful in Sunday Mass. Moreover, the liturgists we interviewed seemed to
summarily dismiss the laity's views on this issue believing that if they (the laity)
would just educate themselves liturgically they would change their minds.

As we noted in chapter 3, many liturgists are part of a liturgical social
movement that has had considerable influence on local parish life. Driving the
outcome of the majority of tabernacles being removed from the sanctuary in
suburban parishes, consequently, are liturgists or local parish professional minis-

ters trained by liturgists. Moreover, removing the tabernacle from the sanctuary is a clear indicator to some that liturgists are on the liberal end of the theological/liturgical continuum, and research in the sociology of religion has shown over and again that clergy and other church professionals are generally more liberal in many church matters than their remaining members.[8] Therefore, if the tabernacle is removed from the sanctuary in a local parish it is likely that there would be increased tension between professional ministers and the ordinary rank-and-file. This is exactly what we found. Laity want to see the tabernacle and professionals wanted to remove it, often increasing the tension between them. It is plausible to speculate, therefore, that liturgists are the main reason why tabernacles are being removed from sanctuaries in suburban parishes because suburban parishes are where liturgists are disproportionately located.

Conclusion

As has been the case with first holy communion and the RCIA, the policies on tabernacle location are transformed as they flow through various situations and social contexts. We initially found that geographic location of parishes, whether a parish was in the city or suburb, exhibited a pattern where suburban parishes were more likely to remove their tabernacles from the main sanctuary of the church and at the same time experience high level of problems with such a move. Aware of the influence of the liturgical social movement, however, we hypothesized that the situation of moving the tabernacle from the sanctuary and that move being highly problematic had more to do with "liturgical presence" of church professionals than it did with geographic location of parishes.[9] And that is exactly what we found: liturgical professionals wanted the tabernacle moved from the main sanctuary and were, for the most part, unmoved by the laity's dislike for such a move. This, of course, resulted in another instance of a lay-professional attitudinal gap where the professionals wanted tabernacle moved and the laity wanted to see it.

In this case with the tabernacle, however, unlike the first holy communion situation or the RCIA situation, the emotional dislike for moving the tabernacle and outright opposition among the laity needs further explanation. Liturgical policies are transformed as they are interpreted by various groups of people in various social situations, but in this case these policies were being interpreted and transformed with an emotional intensity that reached feverish heights.

Durkheim's concept of the "sacred" is one way to help explain the intensity of these divergent views. Durkheim insisted that religion is "real."[10] As he said, the real is evident in the means through which humans come to know and the means begin with human social connectedness and solidarity. The real is ultimately grounded in the social, that is, it is the product of collective doing. Durkheim talks at length about groups of people moving together in ritual, about ritual doing, about assembling, about collective effervescence that emerges when the group assembles, and the physical movements people make when assembled. It is the act of assembling and ritual doing that is real, that produces solidarity, community, the moral conscience, collective effervescence and the sacred.

For Durkheim, then, it is in the actions and movements of assembling and collective doing that are real, and it is in and through these ritual collective doings that people come to ascribe sacredness or sacred power to objects. Hence, the real is not observable if the lone individual is the focus or unit of analysis. Sacredness, wherever it is located, is not real and does not have force or consequences on the group or society if derived by an individual mind. Sacredness is an extraordinary quality and force that only arises within moral communities.

But to drive home the point about the real, Durkheim explains that although sacredness originates as it does, it must be added to the object over and over again through people assembling around it and acting toward it. Sacredness is not inherently permanent in any object. In this case, the tabernacle has derived its sacredness from the human doing of gathering at the tabernacle and praying and singing to it and processing with it through the church and by locating it in a central location. Consequently, the location itself has become sacred through the participants' movements of placing the tabernacle there and repeatedly assembling at that spot to pray. It is at this location, in front of this tabernacle, that collective sentiments, collective passions, collective spiritual enthusiasms, and reinforcements of common faith were enacted. This is why this location is sacred.

With respect to Durkheim's conception of the sacred, the tabernacle is real and sacred to the laity. The consequence of that definition of the situation for the laity is that the tabernacle should be centrally located in the sanctuary. The sanctuary is the holy spot in the church, and the placement of the tabernacle and the altar in that area along with the crucifix and perhaps other religious statues, contributes to the sacredness of the entire sanctuary, tabernacle included. Indeed, to the laity it is like a piling up of sacredness. There is nothing particularly neat and tidy about it. Durkheim even qualified the contrast between the sacred and the profane by acknowledging that there were degrees and ranks of sacredness[11]. The altar and tabernacle, therefore, are not confusing symbols leading the laity to be confused theologically. The close proximity of altar and tabernacle enhances sacredness, for now both altar and tabernacle can be acted toward together. Indeed, for the laity the opposite occurs—the enhancement of active participation and, consequently, an incremental increase in the sacredness of the tabernacle and altar because the people are repeatedly acting toward it. The laity know intuitively and physically of the tabernacle's sacredness for they have collectively and privately assembled around the tabernacle for years and have worshiped and prayed to Christ present there. It is a concrete symbol of Christ's presence to them. It is something material yet sacred that they can relate to and act toward.

Similar to processes creating sacred things, Fred Kniss[12] has argued that cultural resources can influence conflict as much as material or political resources. In his case study of American Mennonites, he notes how cultural resources vary along an abstract—concrete dimension, and how concrete cultural resources are more likely to cause conflict than abstract cultural resources. He says, for example, that cultural resources may take a highly abstract, ideal form and therefore cover a broad range of meanings, increasing their level of abstraction. Consequently, abstract resources are more manipulable and thus more easily mobilized strategically in a conflict than are concrete cultural or political resources. Concrete cultural resources, however, take on more solid form "such as material cultural objects (e.g., church architecture, distinctive attire) or symbolic practices (e.g., liturgical forms)."[13] Kniss describes concrete cultural resources as follows:

> Owing to their less ambiguous nature, concrete cultural resources are less useful strategically because they do not resonate with as broad a range of issues as abstract resources. However, since they are closer to the "surface" of social life, they are more likely to be the object of contention – the resources over which people are inclined to fight. . . . In other words, concrete practices and symbols have more problems with indivisibility than do abstractions. For example, it is difficult to think of someone only partially wearing a black hat. One either wears a piece of clothing or does not. It is possible, on the other hand, to think of a more abstract resource like legitimacy as somewhat divisible. One's legitimate authority over some activities may be reduced while it is retained or increased over other activities.[14]

Kniss's understanding of conflict fits the controversy over the tabernacle. The removal of the tabernacle (legitimated by the principle of active participation—a highly abstract cultural resource) causes such controversy because the tabernacle is a concrete cultural resource and one that is highly salient to the people opposing its removal. The tabernacle is close to the surface of ecclesial social life as well as close to the central identifying Catholic ritual act—the eucharist (high salience). As a result, it is a volatile cultural resource. On the other hand, most of the laity were in agreement with the principle of active participation—an abstract cultural resource. As Kniss would probably predict, professional liturgists were able to convince many laity about the importance of the principle of active participation but not of its use in interpreting where the tabernacle should be located. In other words, the process from principle to its concrete implementation is not a straightforward, simple one to one correspondence. Just because a principle has been taught and even agreed upon does not mean that the people who were educated about it can be easily moved from one point to another. Education is not the only operative dimension in people's lives. Principles must flow through various personal, and in this case, prayerful and emotional contexts, as well as the context of the local community's experience of the tabernacle, ethnic and racial contexts, before a complete understanding of how the location of the tabernacle will be interpreted. In this case, an abstract principle that can mobilize people (active participation) can also cause mini-mutinies when leaders try to apply it to a specific concrete cultural resource. The tabernacle is a concrete, close-to-the-surface, volatile cultural resource that has become imbued with historical, cultural, and personal significance. The articulation of a rational principle alone, that of active participation, is unlikely to convince or persuade others to follow.

These controversies will persist and emotions will continue to run high because the tabernacle is a direct extension of the Mass in that it is the place where the Body of Christ, communion, is reserved, and the Mass or celebration of the eucharist is the fundamental Catholic ritual expressing Catholic identity. Accordingly, it is easy to comprehend how parishioners have come to identify deeply with the tabernacle even though their encounter with it may be brief and only once a week. The tabernacle is related deeply to the central Catholic ritual act and it provides the ordinary Catholic a repertoire of religious behavior, a means to act toward, to bodily do something, to practice with one's body ritual gestures that instill physical and emotional feelings which communicate to them that a worshipful act has been accomplished, and, moreover, that these social acts make them feel like they belong to the Catholic church because they know bodily what to do when they encounter it.

What is at stake, therefore, with respect to the presence or absence of the tabernacle, is a bundle of ritual practices that strike at the heart of Catholic identity. Professional liturgists who want to remove the tabernacle meet resistance because they are seen as diminishing the ordinary pew-dwelling person's religion, which according to Durkheim, are actual practices. Professionals want to advance the theology of the church by clarifying that the Mass is central to Catholic identity, not the tabernacle. But to parishioners this analytic, theological, and rational distinction does not make sense as an embodied perspective. To the pew-dweller it just doesn't feel right. If the professionals continue to remove the tabernacle, then they may well have to wait a very long time for the bodies of ordinary Catholics to catch up with their professional understanding of it. Therefore, given this attitudinal and behavioral gap that exists between professionals and pew-dwellers, it would behoove professionals and laity alike to listen to one another more carefully. This does not mean that professionals should steer a different course, but it does mean that they might reconsider "how" they are steering. As for the laity, this does not mean their discontent and disagreements should not be expressed, but they might consider temporarily suspending them in order to listen and learn specifically more about the tabernacle and generally more about their church. Moreover, collaboration between laity and professionals may just lead to mutual awareness and compromise rather than misunderstandings and uncompromising anger. As Durkheim might have said, the question is not how much education should be given the laity or professionals for that matter, but how their feelings of belonging and solidarity can be enhanced.

Notes

1. Nathan Mitchell, *Cult and Controversy: The Worship of the Eucharist Outside Mass,* (New York: Pueblo Publishing Company, 1982).

2. *General Instruction of the Roman Missal,* National Conference of Catholic Bishops (New York: Catholic Book Publishing Co., 1974 and 1985); *Environment and Art in Catholic Worship,* U.S. Bishops' Committee on the Liturgy (Washington, D.C., 1978) *Code of Canon Law* (Washington D.C., Canon Law Society of America, 1983).

3. Flannery, Austin P. O., ed., *Vatican II: The Concilliar and post Concilliar Documents* (New York: Costello, 1987), 131, #53.

4. Flannery, *Vatican II,* 285, #78.

5. *Instruction on the Worship of the Eucharistic Mystery,* in *Vatican Council II: The Conciliar and Post Conciliar Documents,* ed., Austin Flannery (New York: Costello Publishing Company, 1967 (1987), #54).

6. *Code of Canon Law,* (1983): Canon 938, #2.

7. *General Instruction of the Roman Missal,* (1974): #276.

8. Jeffrey Hadden, *The Gathering Storm in the Churches* (New York: Anchor Books, 1970); Robert Wuthnow, *The Restructuring of American Religion: Society and Faith Since World War II,* (Princeton N.J., Princeton University Press,1988).

9. Most liturgists (75 percent) are in suburban parishes because, first, there are more suburban parishes, and, secondly, suburban parishes are more likely to be able to afford paying a liturgist.

10. Emile Durkheim, *Elementary Forms of Religious Life,* translator Karen Fields (New York: The Free Press, 1912/1995): 2, "If [religion] had not been grounded in the nature of things, in those very things it would have met resistance that it could not have overcome."

11. Karen Fields, translator, *Elementary Forms of Religious Life,* Emile Durkheim (New York: The Free Press, 1912/1995): 306, n7.

12. Fred Kniss, "Ideas and Symbols as Resources in Intrareligious Conflict: The Case of American Mennonites," *Sociology* of Religion 57(1996): 7-23.

13. Fred Kniss, "Ideas and Symbols", 9.

14. Fred Kniss, "Ideas and Symbols", 9.

Chapter 8
Implementing Vatican II

When it became clear that Pope John XXIII wanted a council that would significantly break with the past, rather than merely confirm it, many high ranking officials of the church became suspicious, confused, and even angry. Nevertheless, it is in the Pope's announcement of Vatican II that we can understand his intentions, to the chagrin of many in the curial central administration. A very broad and overriding intention of the Pope was that Vatican II should initiate a "new Pentecost" within the church; that is; it should be another Pentecost like the apostles experienced where the Holy Spirit came upon them and set them on fire with faith. Vatican II, in the Pope's mind, would be another moment of the gift of the Holy Spirit descending on the worldwide church, giving it new life and energy to proclaim the gospel to the world.[1]

This new Pentecost was most clearly articulated in the term "*aggiornamento*," which translates as the church's call to update itself. This became the overall intention or goal of the Pope and most of the bishops attending the proceedings. Vatican II was not about unity *per se*, certainly not about condemning heresies, meeting a specific challenge, or simply reforming some of its teachings. Indeed, this council had no precedent, although many searched the church's history for one. There simply had never been a pastoral council with the aim of updating the church through reading the signs of the times. This sub theme of "reading the signs of the times" was the main method of Vatican II's project of *aggiornamento*, which we find in the document, *Gaudium et spes* (no. 4):

> ...[T]he church has the duty in every age of examining the signs of the times and interpreting them in the light of the gospel, so that it can offer in a manner appropriate to each generation replies to the continual human questioning on the meaning of his life and the life to come and on how they are related. There is a need, then, to be aware of, and to understand, the world in which we live.[2]

Aggiornamento and reading the signs of the times were two dominant and prevailing intentions of the Pope and Vatican II.

An equally important theme of the Council, however, and one that helped Vatican II's thrust of *aggiornamento* hit home, was the principle of active participation, which was most clearly spelled out in the Constitution on the Sacred Liturgy as well as in several other documents. This principle was based on the fundamental theology of the liturgy as a communal act in and through which all members, laity as well as clerics, should embrace an ethos of active engagement. Although other intentions and themes of Vatican II could be enumerated and discussed, we turn now to the reception of these themes of *aggiornamento*, reading the signs of the times, and most especially active participation.

Initially, there were mixed reactions to John XXIII's calling of Vatican II. Some were suspicious, some curious, some elated, and some outright disliked it. It could be said that there was no clear consensus that such a council should take place let alone a consensus on changing some of its central rituals of the church, for example, the eucharist, so that more people (laity) could actively participate in it. But in the end, the majority of bishops at the council affirmed and supported the Constitution on Sacred Liturgy with a vote of 2,147 in favor and only four against.[3]

One of the first suggestions at the Council was that liturgy should be conducted in the vernacular in order for the laity to better understand and thus more actively participate in the liturgy. The proposal to change the norm of having Mass celebrated only in Latin to that of the vernacular was a yearlong process, and which in the end still maintained Latin as the official language of the church but allowed for the use of the vernacular. The heated and lengthy debate over the vernacular exemplifies the dissensus and internal battles that occurred at Vatican II. Generally, however, the principle of active participation spread and prevailed at the Council. Nevertheless, as we have stated in various ways throughout this book, that principle is ambiguous when it comes to concrete pastoral application. It begged the questions such as how active is "active"? What exactly does it mean to participate actively, fully, and consciously? Why, for example, would the vernacular necessarily increase active participation? And what are some of the concrete indicators that measure "active participation"? We believe the intentions of this principle were translucent at best, and could mean different things at different times and places, and therefore were open to interpretation in different ways through different processes. This ambiguity was probably inevitable given the broader goal of *aggiornamento* and a new openness to ideas traditionally closed to Catholicism. This legacy, we believe, still persists and has helped the church embrace a less defensive stance toward other religions and secular society itself. However, we also see and have suggested in this study what we regard as a naïve or even immature sociological posture in that many of the council fathers did not understand or foresee the negative and unanticipated consequences of their decision to embrace the principle of active participation.

The naiveté is most evident in their lack of understanding about how the changes in the liturgy would produce factions among not only clerics and theologians of the church but among the pew-dwellers themselves. Perhaps no one could have predicted such far reaching consequences, for as Bellitto succinctly states:

> The paradigm shifts and new ideas had to be carried out, and that is where, why, and how Vatican II has become a battlefield at the dawn of Christianity's third millennium. . . . That is where Vatican II stands today, with some in the church saying she has moved too far too fast, while others believe she has not moved far enough and indeed has slowed down, if not reversed, her course. But the final legacy of Vatican II must be left to later generations to determine.[4]

Although later generations may come to understand better what took place at Vatican II, we believe, along with others,[5] that the council fathers did not pay close enough attention to what the consequences of their actions might be in legitimizing massive changes in the central ritual practices of the church. In other words, they were naïve in placing excessive hope and transformative power in "ideas," even though these ideas were theologically sound and were constructed for the pastoral benefit of the ordinary Catholic. That is, it seems to us that the bishops assigned more weight and authority to *ideas* about community participation over a community's actual ritual practices that are mechanisms contributing to a sense of community. In reflecting on such changes, we detect the influence of the Enlightenment's emphasis on reason and rational planning overriding the influences of tradition, emotion, and the ritual practices of the church.

Perhaps the clearest sign of reason prevailing over traditional ritual practices is not only in the documents of Vatican II themselves, but in the implementation strategies employed by bishops such as Cardinal Dearden in Detroit. And perhaps the sign *par excellence* of this emphasis on reason can be seen in the massive educational effort that unfolded after Vatican II, which in many of the cases we studied seemed to employ the simplistic idea that education alone can create desired outcomes. The premise was that if the laity would only attend the classes, workshops, and conferences explaining Vatican II and the new liturgy, then they would understand and heartily accept the changes it legitimized. As we have suggested, this is where we believe the bishops were most naïve. Education is not a panacea for social change and it certainly is not the only factor to consider in understanding social change. While education may not have been a conscious strategy in the minds of the bishops, our research and the overall evidence of forty years shows it to have become the dominant mechanism used for liturgical change. The increasing diocesan bureaucratization and professionalization is evidence of this as well as the swiftness in which the changes occurred.

Even though education was their panacea, many now argue there was not "enough education" because the people did not understand the changes, which confirms for us the continuing reliance of church officials on the power of education. For example, Keith Pecklers states in his recent book on the liturgical movement that:

> across the board, there remains a desperate need for further liturgical catechesis [education] as too many of those present on Sunday morning fail to realize that as the Church of Jesus Christ, they are the very body of Christ which they gather to celebrate: thus, the chasm between worship and daily life remains very wide indeed.[6]

But we would argue that it didn't fail because "more education" was needed but because church leaders failed to understand the power of traditional ritual practices.[7]

Religious practices and beliefs, in Emile Durkheim's classic formulation, exist in a mutually sustaining synergy, with practices visually representing beliefs and beliefs conferring significance on practices.[8] With that synergy in mind, it is easy to see that the Vatican II bishops and their theological advisers' "failure" rested in the fact that they could deal only with the element of beliefs and ideas. That is, they could not specify in any detail what a corresponding ritual practice would actually look like in any particular parish. This limitation is common to policy formulation processes and is why any policy, including the Vatican II documents, can only reflect the intentions of the formulators. These ideas and beliefs, however, had to be translated into practices upon reaching local dioceses and parishes. At that point, many church professionals liked the ideas of Vatican II and consequently sought to change the ritual practices with excitement and vigor, whereas most of the laity were resistant to change. Not liking their ritual practices changed, the pew-dwellers indirectly displayed their dislike for the new ideas whether or not they knew their theological content or grounding. Hence, today's internal ecclesial/liturgical culture wars have more to do with the changes in ritual practice than with the changes in ideas.

It could be argued, therefore, that Vatican II tipped the scales in the direction of emphasizing beliefs over ritual practices. Inspired by Enlightenment rational ideals, the new church professionals changed the ritual practice of the Mass, first holy communion, and location of the tabernacle. Moreover, this occurred in a variety of ways, some quite disjunctive. In many conversations we have heard, some priests, for instance, will stop at various points during the Mass to explain to pew-dwellers the meaning of their ritual conduct. It was fairly common, in other words, to experience the Mass being explained or various theories, ideas, narrative accounts being provided by professionals in the form of mini-lectures at various moments throughout the Mass. These mini-lectures varied in content and style, but the underlying assumption was that education would resolve any dissonance or confusion among the faithful.

The mere fact of having to "explain," however, placed greater emphasis and status on the ideas of Vatican II rather than trying to understand what impact these ideas might have on the church's central ritual practices. Bellah, Kertzer, and Warner,[9] following Durkheim, provide a possible explanation as to why this might be the case in that they argue that modern religions, for the most part, focus on belief, leaving ritual practices free to develop in whatever way best serves the interests of the local congregation or pastor. Vatican II created greater variation in ritual practice because as the policies (ideas) flowed downward from Vatican II through various contexts to each parish pastor/priest/lay professional, they interpreted these ideas of Vatican II and implemented them in various ways. The focus on beliefs, consequently, not only allowed local ritual practices to be changed but to be "set free" according to local needs and circumstances.[10]

Transforming Beliefs into Practices

The variation in implementing liturgical beliefs into liturgical practices stemmed from several sources. One source was that the Vatican II documents were general, in many cases rather ambiguous, and were purely theological in character and content. Another was in the different clerical interpretations of the proposals for liturgical change. Francis Mannion, for instance, has identified five "liturgical movements" since the 1970s, ranging from the most progressive, entailing nothing less than a completely new and creative reform, to the most conservative, entailing the contention that Vatican II documents on liturgy were in fundamental error.[11] A third source of variation was in laity awareness of and response to Vatican II proposals. Some parishioners read and studied the documents, but most did not and knew only what they heard from others. Older parishioners who grew up in the traditional Vatican I church were largely resistant to proposed changes, whereas younger members growing up in a Vatican II parish accepted worship practices presented to them and were arguably unaware of any differences from Vatican I practices. And a fourth source of variation is in the content itself of the ritual practices to be changed and the social organization of their translation into actual practices. It is this last source where our empirical materials are the most applicable.

The Detroit Archdiocese clearly existed at the progressive end of the liturgical movements discussed by Francis Mannion. Vatican II was adopted with great enthusiasm and collective effervescence that was in evidence in the diocese through the 1970s. Liturgical training was supported and trained liturgists were hired, those liturgists became part of the "new knowledge class" and actively participated in national liturgical networks, and the diocesan central services grew numerically and became structurally more complex and hierarchical as new offices and personnel were added to carry out the Vatican II agenda. Although the archdiocese is not an organization as such, but rather a network of parishes connected to a central administration, it can be regarded as the overall organizational context of the implementation insofar as it defined the terms and mobilized the resources for the implementation process. The relevant linkages between the central administration and parishes were created by the new offices and professional liturgists. The salience or influence of those linkages, however, varied according to the ritual practices in question and the overall social organization of those practices. We can show that variation by identifying the properties of implementation in each empirical case we have studied.

The conciliar and post-conciliar policy guidelines for the RCIA were the most specific and unambiguous of the three rituals we studied. Those guidelines specified a series of stages and periods of initiation, and in 1988 they became mandatory for parishes implementing the RCIA. Because of the increased formalization and demands of the RCIA, it became necessary to produce specialists trained in the liturgical requirements of the Rite. These specialists, or RCIA coordinators, worked in parishes with cohorts of adults wishing to become Catholics, as well as with the RCIA offices of the diocesan central services. Structurally, this arrangement was organized to ensure uniformity of implementation and to guarantee that the initiation rituals and catechetical processes were liturgically correct. In short, this arrangement was to mobilize the set of intentions of the policy-makers.

The actual implementation of these intentions entailed a variety of accommodations and adjustments to local circumstances. The major context influencing these accommodations and adjustments was whether a parish was located in Detroit or one of its suburbs. In both contexts, coordinators found themselves negotiating the length of time for the RCIA to less than its one-year requirement, but time reductions were significantly shorter in the city parishes. The reason for this difference was twofold. First, city parishes were less likely to have trained liturgists on their staffs, which reduced professional liturgical presence and influence on implementing the RCIA. Second, many adults going through the program in city parishes had "already membership status," meaning that they had been attending services at the parish for many years without officially being initiated into Catholicism. In those cases, city coordinators shortened and simplified the periods and stages of the RCIA on the grounds that the ritual process itself did not contribute to their membership status and commitment to the Catholic faith. In both city and suburban parishes, we found very little if any resistance by the laity to the RCIA process or any of the modifications of its implementation. Although our data are anecdotal in this matter, we think that the lack of resistance was because the laity were largely unaware of the RCIA or its requirements, and even if they were, they held the attitude that it had nothing to do with their own worship practices and that the parish was enhanced by new members regardless of how they became Catholics.

The implementation of policies pertaining to the location of the tabernacle was considerably different than that of the RCIA. The tabernacle has been a central feature in the traditions of Catholic celebration of the Eucharist, and over time tabernacles have come to be impressive objects that visually focused parishioners' ritual conduct. In seeking to transform aspects of Eucharist into a more active and reflective ritual, the authors of the Vatican II documents dealing with the location of the tabernacle struggled with its bearing on the principle of full, active participation. In those struggles, they ended up producing what appear to many as inconsistencies that suggested outright conflicts in the policies. The guidelines variously state that the tabernacle should be located in a "prominent place," in a "distinguished place in a church or oratory," in the "middle of the altar or on a side altar," or "in a chapel suitable for private adoration and prayer." Not only are these guidelines inconsistent, but they use different criteria as guides for where the tabernacle is to be located. Placing it in a chapel, for instance, uses a physical and spatial criterion, while placing it in a "distinguished" or "prominent "place uses a value or honorary criterion. Consequently, whereas the policy is clear that tabernacle location is a matter of new significance calling for diocesan and parish consideration and action, the lines of response to the policy were open to alternative interpretation and therefore varied.

Despite the differences in the degree of specificity and clarity between the policy guidelines pertaining to the RCIA and location of tabernacle, we found in both instances that whether parishes were located in Detroit or one of its suburbs was a major context for implementation. Indeed, the vast majority of city parishes kept their tabernacles in the center of the sanctuary, which the laity regarded as a prominent place, while those parishes moving their tabernacles out of the center of the sanctuary were more likely to be in the suburbs. Our data indicate that the degree of liturgical presence had a major effect on tabernacle location and, as illustrated in our chapter on "Bob the Liturgist," on the extent to which there was parish conflict over the issue. In parishes having permanent trained liturgists, especially if they had a major voice in their worship commissions, our findings indicated that serious problems of decision-making and rancor were common, whether the tabernacle was moved or not. Significant liturgical presence, however, tended to increase the chances that the tabernacle would be moved out of the sanctuary, usually much to the disapproval of the laity. Therefore, we found fractures between the laity, parish professionals, and central services Architectural Review and Environment Committee actions concerning where the tabernacle should be located. The policy, inconsistent in its formulation, was met with patterned yet inconsistent implementation, with professional liturgists having the most influence in the newer suburban parishes.

The first holy communion represented yet a different situation of implementation. Historically, the most significant issue of first holy communion pertained to its place in a sequence of rituals through which children and adolescents born into the Catholic faith would continue the sacramental process toward full initiation into the church. Vatican II reaffirmed the declaration of Pope Pius X that communion should precede confirmation, but the matter of how the first holy communion ritual should be enacted came under question and was given intensified attention. It is therefore curious that none of the conciliar or post-conciliar documents directly addressed or provided guidelines for this particular ritual. Given that silence, any initiatives for revising the ritual could only draw from the general principle of full, active participation of the faithful as a legitimizing policy framework. Combined with the fact that there was no central administrative office specifically devoted to providing guidance on this ritual, parishes wishing to address relevant issues were left to their own devices. The interesting aspect of our data in this case is the extent to which the laity could make their voices heard. Indeed, partly because there were no specific guidelines and partly because laity could read and interpret liturgical statements and thus confront the interpretations put forth by liturgists, we found that the parents involved in adapting the ritual had a significant effect on the outcome. A base of consensus existed between parents and professional liturgists that the ritual was chaotic and in need of revision and clarification, but the parents came to make an argument consistent with the principle of active participation that differed from that of the liturgists and moved the formal vote in the direction of their views. In the end, the first holy communion celebration agreed upon was a hybrid ritual that contained elements of both Vatican I and Vatican II precepts.

The question now becomes whether or not Catholic worship has been transformed as a result of efforts such as the ones we have studied to implement the Vatican II policies on liturgy. The title of our book, *Transforming Catholicism*, strongly suggests that just such a transformation has taken place in the past forty years, and, indeed, there is no doubt that across the board there have been substantial changes in Catholicism and Catholics. While such an assertion seems quite obvious to us and others,[12] it is less clear that the intended transformations of the Constitution on Sacred Liturgy have occurred in the way that the document's framers envisioned. Surely there has been a great deal of activity to implement the liturgical changes, especially in the organization of diocesan and parish offices and in the increased presence of trained liturgists working on behalf of the liturgical proposals. And there has been increased lay participation in parish worship commissions and other venues of lay volunteerism. Has there, however, been a shift from passive to active worship? Have the liturgical changes produced a new sense of the laity and clerics melding together into a new "spiritual community"? Have the changes resulted in a laity that "fully participates" in the sacraments and rituals of worship? If so, what is the evidence for those effects? And if not, what does the evidence in fact suggest?

We certainly can say, based on the studies we have conducted, that lay involvement in liturgical change has varied considerably, ranging from disinterest to overt, active engagement. There is no evidence at all that parishioners in suburban parishes felt that the RCIA contributed to a full, active, conscious assembly, whereas those in city parishes felt that the RCIA actually interfered with active participation, with some threatening to leave their parish if they were forced to go through the entire process as specified by the RCIA documents. There was tremendous lay participation in parishes facing the possibility of their tabernacle being located outside the sanctuary, and our data indicate that there was an increase in awareness and consciousness about the meaning of the tabernacle and its significance for the eucharist. That increased awareness, however, more often than not carried a negative valence in that the laity were opposed to its removal and felt that their worship experiences were diminished rather than collectively enhanced. Moreover, the parents at St. Catherine's parish, in their active engagement with reformulating first holy communion, implicitly raised a fundamental question about the identification of a community of faithful. While the liturgists argued that children sitting and parading together represented a fracture in the spiritual community, the parents saw that arrangement as community itself and that sitting apart from their children did not lessen their pride or love for their children during the ritual.

These data, therefore, suggest that transformed practices do not necessarily contribute to goal achievement. One reason for this is that active engagement can take on the form of overt resistance to goal implementation, and another is that when the goals are implemented these same goals are invariably transformed as accommodations and adjustments are made in local parish situations. Yet a third reason is that the outcomes cannot be measured; only claimed. That is, no one can offer a definitive answer to the questions we posed earlier about how active is "active," how conscious is "conscious," and what constituted "participation." These certainly are iconic and highly valued terms that most if not all Catholics would agree are important to Catholic worship, but they are intrinsically abstract and are relevant to both secular and spiritual communities. Accordingly, when placed inside a policy legitimizing those terms as goals to be achieved and practices to be changed, the situations of their implementation can only become contested and characterized by the interactions of various claimsmakers and stakeholders. This would certainly include the professional liturgists, who have come to acquire a significant measure of influence in defining the liturgical situations of Catholic practices. Not only are their positions sanctioned by Rome, but they are credentialed as the "new knowledge class," supported and energized by their participation in national networks of like-minded liturgical workers, and occupy official positions of decision making at diocesan and parish levels. They are the official interpreters of Vatican II texts, and in many cases there is considerable deference given to their interpretations. However, as we have argued, perhaps like all knowledge classes, they trade primarily on cognitive meanings that they vigorously put forth as truth claims but that suffer a disconnect with ordinary pew-dwellers' understandings of their own faith and interests.

That disconnect is at the heart of our earlier discussion, and drawing on Eric Rothenbuhler's conceptualization of ritual as "appropriately patterned behavior," we can say that the liturgical changes sought by the professionals have resulted in a breakdown in the consensus and tacit understandings of how to worship appropriately. That breakdown is evidenced not only at the site of ritual enactment itself, but also in the cultural and organizational frameworks encasing that enactment. The gradual decline in collective effervescence experienced in the early years of the Vatican II reforms has left only the embedded social organization of diocesan offices enacting a bureaucratic ethos of policy implementation that signifies the disconnect between central administrative services and local parishioners. The rational, managerial approach to implementing the Constitution on the Sacred Liturgy does not have the feel of a collective enterprise tying diocesan interests to parishioner interests, but rather tends to be experienced as a set of administrative mandates serving only the interests of central service professionals. In the course of all this, we find substantial variation in local practices. A few parishes have reverted to Vatican I liturgical practices in that they celebrate the Tridentine Mass where priests face the altar during the Mass, Latin is the primary language, and most of the faithful receive communion on the tongue instead of the hand. Although most pew-dwellers today recognize the general two-part ordered pattern in the Mass, the Liturgy of the Word and Liturgy of the Eucharist, there is tremendous variation in how these parts of the Mass are locally organized and implemented. The music, homilies, intercessions, communion, and entering and exiting the celebration may be experienced very differently depending on which parish one is attending. And, it is not unheard of to find a charismatic Catholic parish in which worship practices are highly expressive and interspersed with testimonials and witnessing. That is, Catholic ritual practices have become more localized, in some cases creating the potential for confusion over how to enact various rituals, in some cases varying from both Vatican I and Vatican II precepts, and in other cases fostering disinterest in participation altogether. Certainly, we feel safe in saying, that localization of ritual enactment challenges the claim commonly expressed before Vatican II, however illusionary it may have been, that the Catholic Mass is the same all over the world, celebrated in the same way everywhere. And, it can be argued, the loss of that illusion diminishes the sense of common participation in a set of common worship practices for many Catholics. This variation and sometimes disillusionment is not only evident among the faithful, as we have shown in the studies presented herein, but also among some sectors of professionals, as Francis Mannion claims.[13] Thus, the transformation of Catholicism surely has occurred in the wake of Vatican II, and just as surely it continues today, but not along any linear trajectory. In some places the Vatican II transformations concerning the liturgy will be put in reverse, in other places they will be placed in stasis, and in yet other situations they will be accelerated. While controversies regarding liturgy will continue, however, we see a new set of issues stemming from Vatican II that may be capturing a great deal of diocesan and parish attention, namely the "new evangelization."

Vatican II and the New Evangelization

As indicated in previous chapters, Vatican II addressed a great many issues, and in addition to those of liturgical change was the challenge to all Catholics to become more active and engaged in their practices as Christians. The ethos of active engagement was at the heart of what Avery Cardinal Dulles regards as the four great constitutions coming out of the Council: the one on the Church (*Lumen Gentium*), on the liturgy (*Sacrosanctum Concilium*), on the Church in the modern world (*Gaudium et Spes*), and on revelation (*Dei Verbum*).[14] While each called for various kinds of change, the change in the metaphor for the laity from the "Body of Christ," while not totally abandoned at Vatican II, to the "People of God" was singularly important, because it signified a transformation in how ordinary Catholics were to regard and conduct themselves. As "People of God," the laity were to embrace the ethos of active engagement and become more participatory and expressive in their worship and everyday lives as Christians. That transformed presence directly involves how religious faith is to be represented and communicated, and is arguably the most relevant to the reformulations found in the complementary documents, *Sacrosanctum Concilium* and *Lumen Gentium*.

If the liturgical reforms ask the laity to be more actively engaged in their worship practices, however, *Lumen Gentium* asks, if not requires, the laity to be even *more* active in their everyday lives as practicing Christians. That increased activity, however, is to focus directly on the perpetuation of the church, for in that document, we read that "The laity are gathered together in the People of God [and] are called upon, as living members, to expend all their energy for the growth of the Church and its continuous sanctification. . . . Through their baptism and confirmation, all are commissioned to that apostolate by the Lord himself."[15] Pope Paul VI, in *Evangelii Nuntiandi (Evangelization in the Modern World, 1975)* reaffirms *Lumen Gentium* by proclaiming that the mandate to spread the "good news" is "the essential mission of the Church." Moreover, the Pope states that this essential mission is new: it is to be "new in expression, new in fervor, new in methods." The "newness" of the new evangelization, in other words, is yet another instance of Vatican II's ethos of active engagement. And in speaking of this new evangelization at the Fourth World Youth Day in 1989, Pope John Paul II underscored that ethos in saying that "It is not enough to discover Christ—you must bring him to others! . . . You must have the courage to speak about Christ, to bear witness to your faith through a lifestyle inspired by the gospel."[16]

Following *Evangelii Nuntiandi*, the United States Bishops formally addressed the Pope's call for a new evangelization, and from their deliberations came the 1992 document, *Go and Make Disciples: A National Plan and Strategy for Catholic Evangelization in the United States*. Overwhelmingly ratified by the

U.S. Bishops, the plan formulated the new evangelization around three major goals: (1) to instill great enthusiasm among Catholics for their faith such that they will share it with others; (2) to invite all people in the U.S. into the Catholic Church; (3) to promote and transform the United States as a Christian nation. These goals were construed as inclusive of everyone in the U.S.–from both practicing and inactive Catholics to Christians of other traditions to non-Christians–with the ethos of active engagement resting at the heart of that inclusion and those goals.[17]

The new evangelization was to entail a Catholic transformation from the faithful merely being "silent witnesses to their faith through living good lives," as Fr. Kenneth Boyak characterizes it, to sharing their faith "by speaking the gospel message clearly and by giving reasons for their Catholic faith." Moreover, this sharing is to be done with great enthusiasm to "enable Catholics to fall more deeply in love with God, thereby becoming more holy."[18] This inclusiveness and enthusiasm thus defines the "newness" of the new evangelization, or, as Bishop Samuel Jacobs puts it, "The call is not just to evangelize, but to evangelize in the power of the Sprit with *new boldness*."[19]

The Detroit Archdiocese appears to be taking this call for the new evangelization seriously, and during the past decade has sought to implement it in a way not unlike its implementation of liturgical changes. In 1992, the diocese created the Office of Evangelization, with the initial goal of making the document "Go and Make Disciples" more accessible to local parishes. That document became the basis for several workshops on evangelization at the diocesan, vicariate, and parish levels. A manual, *Parish Council and Commission Guidelines*, provided directives about parish council and commissions being infused with an evangelization perspective but with no official guideline for establishing evangelization committees *per se* at the parish level. Rather, the intent was that the parish council and commissions would now view all ministry through an evangelization perspective.

A few years later, an initiative was instituted to promote evangelization specifically within Detroit's east side, concentrating on the boundaries of five urban eastside parishes. This effort became known as "Sign Me-Up," which entailed a door-to-door evangelization ministry. This door-to-door ministry did not involve preaching the Gospel, but rather it was a time to greet and invite neighbors to the many Catholic religious opportunities available in the geographical area. By the mid-1990s, there were two priest leaders heading up these diocesan evangelization efforts.

In 2003, these priests were assigned to the newly formed diocesan new evangelization team. The evangelization team continued the "Sign Me Up" program, but began inviting parish members to workshops on evangelization that the team presents at Sacred Heart Major Seminary in Detroit. The seminary (SHMS) is another site in and through which the diocese decided to institutionalize the new evangelization. SHMS made the new evangelization one of its hallmarks by creating the first STL (Licentiate in Sacred Theology, an ecclesiastical degree roughly equivalent to the master's level) graduate degree program in the United States with a concentration on the new evangelization. The STL coordinated a national convocation on the new evangelization in 2006 at St. John's Conference Center in Plymouth, Michigan.

Currently, fifty-five (18 percent) of the parishes in the Detroit Archdiocese have an evangelization committee, with about two-thirds of those involved being women. While at this point the number of parishes implementing the new evangelization is rather low, there has been an increasing number of parishioners attending diocesan-sponsored conferences on the new evangelization. These conferences started in 2003, with eight hundred men attending the men's conference, and has increased to over three thousand in 2006. The women's conference has increased from four hundred in 2004 to twelve hundred in 2006. These conferences have been the largest gatherings of lay men and women in recent diocesan memory, and thus seem to have stirred an interest similar to the early years of Vatican II.

Given this apparent enthusiasm for this new diocesan initiative, coupled with evidence of lay interest in it, we have begun a series of studies asking questions about its implementation, just as we have done concerning the liturgy. We are in the early stages of this research, but can present some data that suggest some similarities and differences to what we found with the liturgy. We have collected data from over 1800 Protestants and Catholics in the Detroit metropolitan area, and among the questions asked were those pertaining to evangelistic activities. Data show that evangelization is not something that Christians in general regularly engage in, with only 15 percent of Protestants and 7 percent of Catholics saying that they are involved in such activities on a weekly basis. When it comes to "representing" the faith, however, the rates go up significantly. A majority of both Protestants and Catholics report that they wear crosses, place religious icons in their homes, cars, and at work, and wear clothing displaying religious symbols. However, members of both denominations seem to decrease their outreach activity in areas requiring high levels of energy or involvement. For instance, while about 60 percent of members report that they say grace at restaurants, and about 40 percent will share their faith at work, only about 5 percent say they hand out religious leaflets, talk door to door about their church, or organize prayer groups at work.

Just as there are no benchmarks for active engagement, there are none for level of enthusiasm in spreading the faith. The call for great enthusiasm and a new boldness in the new evangelization is something very difficult to measure and thus determine when it exists. Our data, however, provide some clues about this matter, and bring us to the question of congregational culture. Our data showed that the two Catholic parishes and two Protestant churches that had the highest participation in outreach activities also had the strongest evangelical traditions and incorporated high levels of expressive worship practices. They also were composed of urban working class and relatively small congregations. One of the Catholic parishes is in Detroit's Westside, is made up of about two hundred and fifty predominately black working class families, and its members are very open to evangelization activities. The other Catholic parish has about three hundred working class and predominantly white families, and has a Catholic charismatic worship style involving spontaneous expressiveness, a charismatic mass, and participatory music. One of the Protestant churches is on Detroit's southside with about one hundred mostly white members. It is a sectarian-like church community, with an expressive, evangelical flavor to Sunday worship, and the other one has about two hundred members, and has had a long and deep evangelical tradition of emotional expressiveness in its worship.

Overall, these data suggest some rather profound differences in the challenges presented by *Sacrosanctum Concilium* and *Lumen Gentium*. The implementation of liturgical change was more of a cognitive shift in worship practices, and was greatly facilitated by the alteration of physical objects such as altars and tabernacles, whereas the implementation of the new evangelization calls for more of an emotional shift and pertains to changes in relationships among the faithful. However, *Lumen Gentium* contains an explicit deficit model of the Catholic laity. As the Pope declared, "It is not enough to discover Christ—you must bring him to others!" And as the United States Bishops have declared, the laity are not nearly enthusiastic enough in sharing the "good news." We speculate that the contention by church leaders that the laity are passive, unenthusiastic, and uninvolved in sharing their faith may well be met by the laity's contention that they in fact *do* share their faith and bring Jesus Christ to others. One of the biggest challenges of the new evangelization, therefore, will be in communicating this deficit model to suburban, affluent parishioners, where congregational culture is more individualistic and instrumental. The most receptive parishes are likely to be those in the inner city areas. However, the problem here is that those receptive parishes are declining in population.

Accordingly, the Catholic new evangelization faces substantial challenges not faced by the new liturgy. First, how are church leaders to communicate the premise that the laity are insufficient Christians without insulting them so much that they turn away from their message? Second, how do they deal with the ecology of faith in which the vast majority of their audience, especially suburban Catholics, arguably will be the least receptive to their message? Third, church leaders should be sensitive to the implications of the distinction between "sharing faith" and "growing the church" and the salience of each to the new evangelization. The challenge of the former is relatively easy if the laity are not asked to drastically alter their lifestyles and that such faith sharing includes all forms of representing their faith. The challenge of the latter, however, involves converting non-Catholics, which creates a tension with ecumenism, and bringing back unchurched and alienated Catholics. Fourth, and last, how will church leaders promote the new evangelization among younger Catholics? James

Davidson recently provided data in the *National Catholic Reporter* that post-Vatican II Catholics have a "more individualistic approach to faith and morals" and are less likely to give credence to the church as mediator between themselves and God. This situation raises the classic question of authority relations and whether church leaders can reasonably expect younger members of the laity to fall in line with church proclamations and initiatives.

While the new liturgy and new evangelization both emanate from the Vatican II call for renewal and consist of challenges to the laity to reinvigorate their faith, the new evangelization may well prove more difficult to implement and sustain. The process of implementation may be quite similar insofar as the obligations of baptism are to be translated into action through the formation of diocesan offices and personnel charged with the task of moving the new liturgy and new evangelization forward through parishes, conferences, workshops and to the parishioners. Beyond those similarities, however, there are rather profound differences. The proposals for liturgical change were formulated to apply to all Catholics in the overt phase of their worship. That is, they were to reconstitute ritual practices that, when combined with appropriate education, would lead the faithful to a new sharing and collective spiritual experience. But unlike the liturgy, whose proposals were non-voluntary in their structure, the new evangelization workers should be aware that enthusiasm for one's faith can be neither mandated nor extracted from the laity. Enthusiasm comes from within the person, is born of commitment, and must find its place with other commitments that define everyday life. Consequently, evangelization teams that criticize the laity for what they might regard as inadequate vigor or boldness in representing their faith to others may well find themselves without an audience. Moreover, the liturgical and evangelization agendas for renewal are not isomorphic and are even conflictual in some ways. Liturgists seek to promote worship practices conducted in the proper way, while evangelization workers seek to promote worship conducted in a more expressive way. It is highly probable that these two modes of worship in their idealized form cannot coexist in the same instance of ritual behavior.[20] Therefore, like the liturgists, evangelization workers must realize that "active participation" is a moving target with no definitive markers that might signal successful evangelization efforts, and they would do well to accept with gratitude the faith and commitments the laity bring to the church. Therein lies a fundamental irony of implementation, namely that evangelization teams must develop a culture of invitation for the laity, Catholic and non-Catholic alike, rather than a culture of strategic planning justified in the church's positioning the laity as having an obligation to be enthusiastic about their faith.

Notes

1. Christopher M. Bellitto. *The General Councils: A History of the Twenty-One Church Councils from Nicaea to Vatican II*, (New York: Paulist Press, 2002).

2. *Gadium et spes* (No 4), in *Vatican Council II: The Conciliar and Post Conciliar Documents*, ed. Austin Flannery (New York: Costello Publishing Company, 1987).

3. Annibale Bugnini. *The Reform of the Liturgy: 1948-1975* (Collegeville: The Liturgical Press, 1990), 37.

4. Bellitto, *The General Councils*, 145-6.

5. Kieran Flanagan, *Sociology and Liturgy: Re-presentations of the Holy*, (New York: St. Martin's Press, 1991), and David Torevell, *Losing the Sacred: Ritual, Modernity and Liturgical Reform*, (London: T&T Clark International, A Continuum Imprint, 2000).

6. Keith F. Pecklers. *Worship: A Primer in Christian Ritual* (Collegeville: The Liturgical Press, 2003), 116. Similarly, in 2003 the following conversation occurred while doing field research with a parish Director of Religion Education in charge of first holy communion: Researcher: "what do you mean when you say 'here we go again' about first holy communion." DRE: "well, it means I have to work with the parents more because they don't know a thing about the eucharist, unbelievable. They just don't get it. I mean they need to know what they are celebrating . . . and why they are celebrating. So I just have to do more education with the parents and so I'm thinking about having more parent education sessions next year. The parents get that it is important but they emphasize the wrong thing; it is about dresses and even limos now, do you believe it, they get their kid a limo, but they don't even know that it is a sacrament of initiation." Researcher: "Do they sit with their parents?" DRE: "yes, but it should be at the regular Sunday Mass, but the priest insists it be a separate Mass because there would just be too many people and we would never get them all into church. But they should sit with their parents, that is who they go to church with and that is why I need to work with the parents more to get them to understand this sacrament and its transformative power and grace."

7. For a similar argument, see David Torevell, *Losing the Sacred*.

8. Emile Durkheim, *The Elementary Forms of Religious Life*, (New York: Free Press, 1912/1965).

9. Robert Bellah, "Durkheim and Ritual," in *The Cambridge Companion to Durkheim*, eds. Jeffrey C. Alexander and Philip Smith, (New York: Cambridge University Press, 2005), 183-210; David I. Kertzer, *Ritual, Politics, and Power*, (New Haven: Yale University Press, 1988); and Stephen R. Warner, *A Church of Our Own: Disestablishment and Diversity in American Religion*, (New Brunswick: Rutgers University Press, 2005).

10. A simple example of how local practices have been set free can be illustrated by my (Michael McCallion) pastor who "tells us" before Mass begins to shake hands and say hello to our neighbor next to us and behind us. Several parishioners have told me how silly they feel when they are told to do this. They are not sure why but they are uncomfortable with the practice. Partly, I think it is because some have already said hello and hence find it a little embarrassing. For myself, I find it very parent to child if you will, that is, I often tell my son Kevin something similar like, "Kevin, remember to say hello to Grandpa and shake his hand." So, many feel silly because a ritual practice that adults use to socialize their children is now being imposed on them – adults. It simply does not

feel right in one's body, regardless if it is understood as a form of parent to child communication. It is in their bones, in their body, and so in doing it, it feels odd because it is not a normal, regular, adult social practice. The point, however, is that ritual practices have been set free at the local level according to the whim of those in charge. Consequently, a decrease in ritual solidarity occurred at the local parish level and at the more general level of the church universal after Vatican II (indeed, one still hears today, "I use to be able to go anywhere in the world and the Mass was the same – I could at least follow along"). Inevitably conflicts arose because practices were being changed not because of a change in ideas *per se*, although there was confusion/anomie over the ideas as well. What many pew-dwellers complained about was the lack of "ritual sameness" whereas as most professionals complained about the peoples' lack of understanding and their need for more education.

11. Francis M. Mannion, "Agendas for Liturgical Reform," *America*, 175 (1996): 9-16.

12. Many scholars have written of these changes, including Andrew Greeley, *The Catholic Revolution*, (Berkeley: University of California Press, 2004); Peter Steinfels, *A People Adrift: The Crisis of the Roman Catholic Church in America*, (New York: Simon and Schuster, 2005); James Davidson and Andrea Williams, "Megatrends in 20th Century American Catholicism," *Social Compass* 44 (1997): 507-27; and Joseph Gremillion and Jim Castelli, *The Emerging Parish: The Notre Dame Study of Catholic Life Since Vatican II*, (San Francisco: Harper & Row Publishers, 1987).

13. These tensions still exist among professionals as this interview in 2004 with a professional Archdiocesan liturgist exemplifies: Researcher: "so the Tridentine Mass is going to happen?" Liturgist: (shaking his head disapprovingly) "yea, and I betch ya a large number of kooks show up. . . . Yea, and like that is going to bring back 'mystery.' That is all I hear when these people complain, there is no mystery in the Mass anymore, that's all I hear – mystery, mystery, mystery. But they just are not clear on what the eucharist is all about. If they could just fully participate in the Vatican II liturgy they would find life and meaning and mystery. . . . And yes I hear that too about lack of statues, yea, as if statues bring mystery, I don't get it. The idea of actively participating around the one altar is the focus and they don't get or don't want to get it and so all this talk about statues and stuff is coming back. I just think it is a step backwards."

14. Avery Dulles, "From Ratzinger to Benedict," *First Things* 160 (2006): 24-9.

15. *Lumen Gentium*, no. 17.

16. Cited in Bishop William Houck, "Introduction," *John Paul II and the New Evangelization*, eds., Ralph Martin and Peter Williamson, (San Francisco: Ignatius Press, 1995), 21.

17. The Bishops' document is nicely discussed by Fr. Kenneth Boyack, "Go and Make Disciples: The United States Bishops' National Plan for Catholic Evangelization." *John Paul II and the New Evangelization*, eds., Ralph Martin and Peter Williamson (San Francisco: Ignatius Press, 1995), 71-85.

18. Fr. Kenneth Boyack, "Go and Make Disciples," 78, 80.

19. Bishop Samuel Jacobs, "How Must Catholics Evangelize? Evangelization and the Power of the Holy Spirit," *Pope John Paul II and the New Evangelization*, eds., Ralph Martin and Peter Williamson (San Francisco: Ignatius Press, 1995), 61.

20. The incompatibilities we mention here are supported by interviews we have conducted with liturgists about the new evangelization. One liturgist, reacting to a presentation about the new evangelization stated, "Who is that guy? I mean, he went on and on

about Jesus this and Jesus that! I mean, what is all this Jesus talk and being committed to the Lord and having a personal relationship with Jesus? I don't know what is going on over there. It seems very conservative to me and maybe even pre-Vatican II." Another liturgist commented, "They operate out of a different ecclesiology. It seems to me that they are very conservative and even backward looking in that they offer these conferences for men and it is all about being a soldier for Christ. My God, that is pre-Vatican II language, that militaristic emphasis! Who do they think they are forming and for what purpose—to go and fight for God? I don't know…very strange in my estimation."

Bibliography

Abbott, Andrew. "Reflections on the Future of Sociology." *Contemporary Sociology* 29 (2000): 286-300.

Albergio, Guiseppe. "The Christian Situation After Vatican II," Pp. 1-23 in *The Reception of Vatican II*, edited by Guiseppe Albergio, Jean-Pierre Jossua, and Joseph Komonchak. Washington, D.C.: The Catholic University Press of America, 1987.

Barker, Roger and Herbert Wright. *One Boy's Day*. New York: Harper and Row, 1951.

Becker, Howard, and Blanche Geer. "The Fate of Idealism in Medical School." *American Sociological Review* 23 (1958): 50-6.

Bellah, Robert N. "Durkheim and Ritual," Pp. 183-210 in *The Cambridge Companion to Durkheim*, edited by Jeffrey C. Alexander and Philip Smith. New York: Cambridge University Press, 2005.

Bellitto, Christopher M. *The General Councils: A History of the Twenty-One Church Councils from Nicaea to Vatican II*. New York: Paulist Press, 2002.

Berger, Bennett. *Working Class Suburbs*. Berkeley: University of California Press, 1960.

Bertaux, Daniel. *Biography and Society: The Life History Approach in the Social Sciences*. London: Sage, 1981.

Beuchler, Steven. "Beyond Resource Mobilization? Emerging Trends in Social Movement Theory." *The Sociological Quarterly* 34 (1993): 217-35.

Bianchi, E., and Ruether R. R. eds. *A Democratic Catholic Church: The Reconstruction of Roman Catholicism*. New York: Crossroads, 1992.

Bjorklund, Diane. *Interpreting the Self: Two Hundred Years of American Biography*. Chicago: University of Chicago Press, 1998.

Blumer, Herbert, "Society as Symbolic Interaction." Pp. 179-92 in *Human Behavior and Social Processes*, edited by Arnold Rose. Boston: Houghton-Mifflin, 1962.

——*Industrialization as an Agent of Social Change*. Hawthorne, NY: Aldine de Gruyter, 1990.

Botte, Bernard. *From Silence to Participation: An Insider's View of Liturgical Renewal*. Washington, D.C.: The Liturgical Press, 1988.

Boyack, Kenneth. "Go and Make Disciples: The United States Bishops' National Plan for Catholic Evangelization," Pp. 71-85 in *John Paul II and the New Evangelization*, edited by Ralph Martin and Peter Williamson, San Francisco: Ignatius Press, 1995.

Bridger, Jeffrey, and David R. Maines. "Narrative Structures and Detroit Church Clos-
    ings." *Qualitative Sociology* 21(1988): 319-40.
Bromley, David G. "A Tale of Two Theories: Brainwashing and Conversion as Compet-
    ing Political Narratives." Web page article, 2000.
Bromley, David G., and Bruce Busching. "Understanding the Structure of Contractual
    and Covenantal Social Relations: Implications for the Sociology of Religion." *So-
    ciological Analysis* 49 (1988), 15-32.
Bugnini, Annibale. *The Reform of the Liturgy: 1948-1974*. Collegeville: The Liturgical
    Press, 1990.
Carroll, Colleen. *The New Faithful: Why Young Adults are Embracing Christian Ortho-
    doxy*. Chicago: Loyola Press, 2002.
Casanova, Jose. *Public Religions in the Modern World*. Chicago: University of Chicago
    Press. 1994.
Capps, Donald, and Richard K. Fenn. *Individualism Reconsidered: Readings Bearing on
    the Endangered Self in Modern Society*. Center for Religion, Self, and Society,
    Princeton Theological Seminary, Monograph Series, Number 1, New Jersey: A & A
    Printing Co., Inc., 1992.
Clemens, Paul. *Made in Detroit: A South of 8 Mile Memoir*. New York: Doubleday,
    2005.
Code of Canon Law. Canon Law Society of America, Washington, D.C. 1983.
Coleman, John. *The Evolution of Dutch Catholicism, 1958-1974*. Berkeley: University of
    California Press, 1978.
Collins, Randall. "Situational Stratification: A Micro-Macro Theory of Inequality." *So-
    ciological Theory* 18 (2000): 17-43.
Coriden, James. *The Parish in Catholic Tradition: History, Theology, and Canon Law*.
    New York: Paulist Press, 1997.
Coughlin, Charles. *Father Coughlin's Radio Discourses*. The Radio League of the Little
    Flower, 1932.
Darden, Joe, Richard Child Hill, June Thomas, and Richard Thomas. *Detroit: Race and
    Uneven Development*. Philadelphia: Temple University Press, 1987.
Davidson, James, and Williams, Andrea. "Megatrends in 20th Century American Catholi-
    cism," *Social Compass* 44 (1997): 507-27.
DeLambo, David. *Lay Parish Ministers: A Study of Emerging Leadership*. New York:
    National Pastoral Life Center, 2005.
Denzin, Norman. *Interpretive Biography*. Newbury Park, CA: Sage, 1989.
Dillon, Michele. *Catholic Identity: Balancing Reason, Faith, and Power*. Cambridge:
    Cambridge University Press, 1999.
Dinges, William D. "Ritual Conflict as Social Conflict: Liturgical Reform in the Roman
    Catholic Church." *Sociological Analysis* 48 (1987): 138-57.
Dolan, Jay P. *In Search of American Catholicism: A History of Religion and Culture in
    Tension*. Oxford: Oxford University Press, 2002.
Dornfeld, Tim. "Rethinking Children's Liturgy of the Word." *Modern Liturgy*
    21(1990):14-6.
Douglas, Mary. *Natural Symbols: Explorations in Cosmology*. New York: Vintage
    Books, 1970.
Dulles, Avery. *The Reshaping of Catholicism: Current Challenges in the Theology of
    Church*. San Francisco: Harper and Row, 1988.

———. "From Ratzinger to Benedict." *First Things* 160 (2006): 24-9.

Dunlap, Judith. "First Communion: A Teachable Moment." *Church*, Spring (1995): 44-5.

Durkheim, Emile. *The Elementary Forms of Religious Life*. New York: Free Press: 1912/1965.

———. *The Elementary Forms of Religious Life*. Translated by Karen Fields, New York: Free Press, 1912/1995.

Ebaugh, Helen Rose. "Vatican II and the Revitalization Movement," Pp. 3-19 in *Religion and Social Order: Vatican II and U.S. Catholicism*, edited by Helen Rose Ebaugh. Greenwich, CT: JAI Press, 1991.

Elliott, Peter. *The Liturgical Question Box*. San Francisco: Ignatius Press, 1998.

Estes, Carroll, and Beverly Edmonds. "Symbolic Interaction and Policy Analysis." *Symbolic Interaction* 4 (1981): 74-86.

Fine, Gary Alan. "Public Narration and Group Culture: Discerning Discourse in Social Movement," in *Social Movements and Culture*, edited by Hank Johnston and Bert Klandermans. Minneapolis: University of Minnesota Press, 1995.

Fine, Gary Alan, and Sherryl Kleinmann. "Network and Meaning: An Interactionist Approach to Structure." *Symbolic Interaction* 6(1983): 97-110.

Flanagan, Kieran. *Sociology and Liturgy: Re-presentations of the Holy*. New York: St. Martin's Press, 1991.

Flannery, Austin P. O., ed. *Vatican II: The Concilliar and post Concilliar Documents*. New York: Costello, 1987.

Gans, Herbert. *The Urban Villagers*. New York: The Free Press, 1962.

Gecas, Viktor, and Peter Burke. "Self and Identity," Pp. 41-67 in *Sociological Perspectives on Social Psychology*, edited by Karen Cook, Gary Alan Fine, and James House. Boston: Allyn and Bacon, 1995.

Geist, Patricia, and Monica Hardesty. *Negotiating the Crisis: DRG's and the Transformation of Hospitals*. Hillsdale, NY: Lawrence Erlbaum, 1992.

General Instruction of the Roman Missal. New York: Catholic Book Publishing, 1975.

Gensler, Gael. "The Rite of Christian Initiation Adapted for Children: First Steps." *Catechumenate* (May, 1990): 15-9.

Giddens, Anthony. *The Constitution of Society*. Berkeley: University of California Press, 1984.

Glaser, Barney, and Anselm Strauss. *Time for Dying*. Chicago: Aldine, 1968.

Goffman, Erving. *Frame Analysis*. New York: Harper and Row, 1974.

Gottshalk, L., Clyde Kluckhohn, and Robert Angell. *The Use of Personal Documents in History, Anthropology, and Sociology*. New York: Social Science Research Council, 1945.

Greeley, Andrew. *The Catholic Revolution*. Berkeley: University of California Press, 2004.

———. "Habits of the Head." *Society* (May/June 1992).

Gremillion, Joseph, and Jim Castelli. *The Emerging Parish: The Notre Dame Study of Catholic Life Since Vatican II*. San Francisco: Harper & Row, Publishers, 1987.

Hadden, Jeffrey. *The Gathering Storm in the Churches*. New York: Anchor Books, 1970.

Hall, Peter. "Interactionism and the Study of Social Organization." *The Sociological Quarterly* 28 (1987): 1-22.

———. "The Consequences of Qualitative Analysis for Sociological Theory: Beyond the Microlevel." *The Sociological Quarterly* 36 (1995): 397-425.

———. "Metapower, Social Organization, and the Shaping of Social Action." *Symbolic Interaction* 20 (1997): 397-418.

Hall, Peter, and Patrick McGinty. "Policy as the Transformation of Intentions: Producing Program from Statute." *The Sociological Quarterly* 38 (1997): 439-67.

Hargrove, Barbara. "Religion, Development, and Changing Paradigms." *Sociological Analysis* 49(1988): 33-48.

Havermann, Heather. "The Future of Organizational Sociology: Forging Ties Among Paradigms." *Contemporary Sociology* 29 (2000): 476-86.

Hays, Sharon. "Structure and Agency and the Sticky Problem of Order." *Sociological Theory* 12 (1994): 57-72.

Hedstrom, Peter, Richard Dandell, and Charlotta Stern, "Mesolevel Networks and the Diffusion of Social Movements." *American Journal of Sociology* 106 (2000): 173-208.

Henson, Bruce, and Peter Hall. "Linking Performance Evaluation and Career Ladder Programs in One School District." *Elementary School Journal* 93 (1993): 323-53.

Hitchcock, James. *The Decline and Fall of Radical Catholicism*. New York: Herder and Herder, 1971.

Houck, William. "Introduction," Pp. 17-24 in *John Paul II and the New Evangelization*, edited by Ralph Martin and Peter Williamson. San Francisco: Ignatius Press, 1995.

Jacobs, Samuel. "How Must Catholics Evangelize? Evangelization and the Power of the Holy Spirit," Pp. 60-70 in *Pope John Paul II and the New Evangelization*, edited by Ralph Martin and Peter Williamson, San Francisco: Ignatius Press, 1995.

Johnson, Maxwell E. *The Rites of Christian Initiation of Adults: Their Evolution and Interpretation*. Collegeville: The Liturgical Press, 1999.

Johnson, Paul. *Pope John Paul II and the Catholic Restoration*. Ann Arbor, MI: Servant Publications, 1981.

Kavanagh, Aidan. *The Shape of Baptism: The Rite of Christian Initiation of Adults*. New York: Pueblo Publishing Co, 1978.

———. "Catechesis: Formation in Stages." Pp. 36-51 in *The Baptismal Mystery and the Catechumenate*, edited by Michael W. Merriman. New York: The Church Hymnal Corporation, 1990.

———. "Christian Initiation: Tactics and Strategy," Pp.1-6 in *Made, Not Born: New Perspectives on Christian Initiation and the Catechumenate*, edited by The Murphy Center for Liturgical Research. Notre Dame: University of Notre Dame Press, 1974.

Kelly, George A. *The Battle for the American Church*. New York: Doubleday, 1981.

Kertzer, David I. *Ritual, Politics, and Power*. New Haven: Yale University Press, 1988.

Kniss, Fred. "Ideas and Symbols as Resources in Intrareligious Conflict: The Case of American Mennonites." *Sociology of Religion* 57(1996): 7-23.

Koenker, Ernest. *The Liturgical Renaissance in the Roman Catholic Church*. St. Louis: Concordia Publishing House, 1966.

Leege, David C. "Parish Life Among the Leaders," in *Notre Dame Study of Catholic Parish Life, Report No. 9*. Notre Dame, IN.: Institute for Pastoral and Social Ministry, 1986.

Leonard, John-Brooks. "Children of the Promise: A Place in the Assembly." *Assembly* 17 (1991): 524-26.

Lewinski, Ronald. "Celebrating First Communion." *Liturgy 90*, January (1990).

Lofland, John. *Social Movement Organizations: Guide to Research on Insurgent Realities*. New York: Aldine de Gruyter, 1996.

Maines, David R. "In Search of Mesostructure: Studies in the Negotiated Order."*Urban Life* 11 (1982): 267-79.

———. "The Social Construction of Meaning." *Contemporary Sociology* 29 (2000): 577-84.

———. "Life Histories and Narratives." Pp. 1633-9 in *Encyclopedia of Sociology*, edited by Edgar Borgatta and Rhonda Montgomery. New York: Macmillan, 2000.

———. "Pragmatism." Pp. 2217-24 in *Encyclopedia of Sociology*, edited by Edgar Borgatta and Rhonda Montgomery. New York: Macmillan, 2000.

———. *The Faultline of Consciousness: A View of Interactionism in Sociology*. Hawthorne, NY: Aldine de Gruyter, 2001.

———. "Narrative's Moment and Sociology's Phenomena: Toward a Narrative Sociology." *The Sociological Quarterly* 34(1993): 17-38.

Maines, David R., and Jeffrey Bridger. "Narrative, Community, and Land Use Decisions." *The Social Science Journal* 29(1992): 283-92.

Maines, David R., Noreen Sugrue, and Michael Katovich. "The Sociological Import of G.H. Mead's Theory of the Past." *American Sociological Review* 48(1983): 151-73.

Maines, David R., and Michael J. McCallion. "Evidence of and Speculation on Catholic *de facto* Congregationalism," *Review of Religious Research* 46(2004): 92-101.

Maldonado, Luis. "Liturgy as Communal Enterprise," Pp. 309-21 in *The Reception of Vatican II*, edited by Guiseppe Albergio, Jean-Pierre Jossua, and Joseph Komonchak. Washington, D.C.: The Catholic University of America Press, 1987.

Mannion, Francis M. "Agendas for Liturgical Reform," *America*, 175 (1996): 9-16.

Massa, Mark S. *Catholics and American Culture*. New York: The Crossroad Publishing Co., 1999.

May, William E. and Kenneth D. Whitehead, eds., *The Battle for the Catholic Mind: Catholic Faith and Catholic Intellect in the Work of the Fellowship of Catholic Scholars 1978-95*. South Bend, Indiana: St. Augustine's Press, 2001.

McCallion, Michael J. *The Rite of Christian Initiation of Adults in City and Suburban Parishes in the Archdiocese of Detroit*. Doctoral Dissertation, Detroit: Wayne State University, 1996.

McCallion, Michael J., and David R. Maines. "Spiritual Gatekeepers: The RCIA and the Problem of Time." *Symbolic Interaction* 25(2002): 289-302.

———. "Clergy, Laity, and the Liturgy." *Antiphon* 3(1998): 18-21, 24.

McGreevy, John T. *Catholicism and American Freedom: A History*. New York: W.W. Norton and Company, 2003.

———. *Parish Boundaries: The Catholic Encounter with Race in the Twentieth-Century Urban North*. Chicago: University of Chicago Press, 1996.

McManus, Frederick R. "Vision: Voices from the Past." Pp. 308-22 in *National Meeting Addresses 1990-1995*, edited by Michael Spillane. Washington, D.C.: Federation of Diocesan Liturgical Commissions, 1996.

McSweeney, William. *Roman Catholicism: The Search for Relevance*. New York: St. Martin's Press, 1980.

Mead, George Herbert. *Mind, Self and Society*. Chicago: University of Chicago Press, 1934.

Meyer, John, and Ronald Jepperson. "The 'Actors' of Modern Society: The Cultural Construction of Social Agency." *Sociological Theory* 18 (2000): 100-19.

Mills, C. Wright. *The Sociological Imagination*. New York: Oxford University Press, 1959.

Mitchell, Nathan D. "Powers of Persuasion." *America*, October (1999): 12-5.

————. *Cult and Controversy: The Worship of the Eucharist Outside Mass*. New York: Pueblo Publishing Company, 1982.

Morris, Charles R. *American Catholic: The Saints and Sinners Who Built America's Most Powerful Church*. New York: Times Books Random House, 1997.

Murnion, Philip J., and David DeLambo. *Parishes and Parish Ministries: A Study of Parish Lay Ministry*. New York: National Pastoral Life Center, 1999.

Neuhaus, Richard John. *The Catholic Moment*. New York: Harper and Row, 1987.

Pare, George. *The Catholic Church in Detroit, 1701-1888*. Detroit: Gabriel Richard Press, 1951.

Park, Robert. "Human Migration and the Marginal Man." *American Journal of Sociology* 33 (1928): 881-93.

Pecklers, Keith F. *Worship: A Primer in Christian Ritual*. Collegeville: The Liturgical Press, 2003.

Perko, Michael. *Catholic and American: A Popular History*. Huntington, IN: Our Sunday Visitor Publishing Division, 1989.

Portes, Alejandro. "The Hidden Abode: Sociology as Analysis of the Unexpected." *American Sociological Review* 65 (2000): 1-18.

Pottmeyer, Hermann. "A New Phase in the Reception of Vatican II: Twenty Years of Interpretation of the Council," Pp. 27-43 in *The Reception of Vatican II*, edited by Guiseppe Albergio, Jean-Pierre Jossua, and Joseph Komonchak. Washington, D.C.: The Catholic University of America Press, 1987.

Reger, Jo. "Organizational 'Emotion Work' Through Consciousness-Raising: An Analysis of a Feminist Organization." *Qualitative Sociology* 27 (2004): 205-22.

Rendler, Elaine. "Liturgy 2000." (paper presented to Department of Parish Life, Archdiocese of Detroit, May 1995).

Riemann G., and F. Schutze, "Trajectory as a Basic Theoretical concept for Analyzing Suffering and Disorderly Social Processes." Pp. 333-57 in *Social Organization and Social Processes: Essays in Honor of Anselm Strauss*, edited by David Maines. Hawthorne, NY: Aldine de Gruyter, 1991.

Rite of Christian Initiation of Adults. Chicago: Liturgy Training Publications, 1988.

Rothenbuhler, Eric. *Ritual Communication: From Everyday Conversation to Mediated Ceremony*. Thousand Oaks, CA: Sage, 1998.

Schoenherr, Richard A. *Goodbye Father: The Celibate Male Priesthood and the Future of the Catholic Church*. Oxford: Oxford University Press, 2002.

Searle, Mark. *Christening: The Making of Christians*. Collegeville: The Liturgical Press, 1980.

————. "Issues in Christian Initiation: Uses and abuses of the RCIA." *The Living Light* 22 (1986): 199-214.

Sewell, William. "A Theory of Structure: Duality, Agency, and Transition." *American Journal of Sociology* 98 (1992): 1-29.

Shepherd, Lancelot. *The Liturgical Movement*, trans. New York: Hawthorn Books, 1964.

Smith, Philip, and Jeffrey C. Alexander. "Introduction: The New Durkheim," Pp. 1-40 in *The Cambridge Companion to Durkheim*, edited by Jeffrey C. Alexander and Philip Smith, Cambridge: Cambridge University Press, 2005.

Snow, David, A. Rochford, E. Burke, Steven Worden, and Robert Benford. "Frame Alignment Processes, Micromobilization, and Movement Participation." *American Sociological Review* 51 (1986): 464-81.

Snow, David, and Robert Benford. "Ideology, Frame Resonance, and Participant Mobilization." *International Social Movement Research* 1 (1988): 197-217.

Steinfels, Peter. *A People Adrift: The Crisis of the Roman Catholic Church in America.* New York: Simon and Schuster, 2005.

Stone, Gregory P. "Appearance and the Self: A Slightly Revised Version." Pp. 187-202 in *Social PsychologyThrough Symbolic Interaction*, edited by Gregory P. Stone and Harvey A. Farberman. New York: Wiley and Sons, 1981.

Strauss, Anselm. *Anguish.* San Francisco: The Sociology Press, 1971.

———. *Continual Permutations of Action.* Hawthorne, NY: Aldine de Gruyter, 1991.

Sugrue, Thomas J. *The Origins of the Urban Crisis: Race and Inequality in Postwar Detroit.* Princeton: Princeton University Press, 1996.

Swart, William J. "The League of Nations and the Irish Question: Master Frames, Cycles of Protest, and Master Frame Alignment." *The Sociological Quarterly* 36 (1995): 465-81.

Swidler, Ann. "Culture in Action: Symbols and Strategies," *American Sociological Review* 51 (1986): 273-86.

"The Emerging Layman." *The National Catholic Reporter.* February 10, 1965: 12.

The Liturgy Documents: Volume 1 A Parish Resource. Chicago: Liturgy Training Publications, 1997.

Tentler, Leslie Woodcock. *Seasons of Grace: A History of the Catholic Archdiocese of Detroit.* Detroit: Wayne State University Press. 1990.

Thomas, William I., and Florian Znaniecki. *The Polish Peasant in Europe and America.* Chicago: University of Chicago Press, 1918.

Torevell, David. *Losing the Sacred: Ritual, Modernity and Liturgical Reform.* London: T & T Clark International, A Continuum imprint, 2000.

Travisano, Richard V. "Alternation and Conversion as Qualitatively Different Transformations." Pp. 594-606 in *Social Psychology Through Symbolic Interaction*, edited by Gregory Stone and Harvey Farberman. Toronto: Xerox College Publishing, 1970.

Ulmer, Jeffery. *The Social Worlds of Sentencing.* Albany, NY: SUNY Press, 1997.

Varacalli, J. *Toward the Establishment of Liberal Catholicism in America.* Lanham, MD: University Press of America, 1983.

Von Hildebrand, Dietrich. *Trojan Horse in the City of God.* Chicago: Franciscan Herald Press, 1967.

Warner, Stephen R. "Work in Progress: Toward a New Paradigm for the Sociological Study of Religion in the United States." *American Journal of Sociology* 98(1993): 1044-93.

———. *A Church of Our Own: Disestablishment and Diversity in American Religion.* New Brunswick: Rutgers University Press, 2005.

Warren, Donald I. *Radio Priest: Charles Coughlin, The Father of Hate Radio.* New York: The Free Press, 1996.

Weaver, Mary Jo, and Appleby, Scott R. Editors, *Being Right: Conservative Catholics in America.* Bloomington, IN: Indiana University Press, 1995.

Widick, B.J. *Detroit: City of Race and Class Violence.* Detroit: Wayne State University Press, 1989.

Wilde, Melissa, Jo. "How Culture Mattered at Vatican II: Collegiality Trumps Authority in the Council's Social Movement Organizations." *American Sociological Review* 69 (2004): 576-602.

Wilhelmsen, Frederick. "Catholicism is Right, So Why Change It?" *Saturday Evening Post* (July 1967): 12.

Wuthnow, Robert. *Meaning and Moral Order: Explorations in Cultural Analysis.* Berkeley and Los Angeles: University of California Press. 1987.

———. *The Restructuring of American Religion: Society and Faith Since World War II.* Princeton, NJ: Princeton University Press, 1988.

Yamane, David, and MacMillen, Sarah. *Real Stories of Christian Initiation: Lessons for and from the RCIA.* Collegeville: Liturgical Press, 2006.

Index

About the Authors

Michael J. McCallion holds the Rev. William Cunningham Chair of Catholic Social Analysis at Sacred Heart Major Seminary and is the Director of the Office of Pastoral Resources and Research in the Department of Parish Life and Services in the Archdiocese of Detroit. He received his Ph.D. in sociology from Wayne State University and his M.A. in liturgy/theology from the University of Notre Dame. He has taught a variety of sociology of religion courses at Wayne State University, Oakland University, and Sacred Heart Major Seminary. His academic publications have appeared in the *Review of Religious Research, Journal of Contemporary Ethnography, Symbolic Interaction, Contemporary Sociology, Antiphon: A Journal for Liturgical Renewal,* and the *Encyclopedia of Sociology.* His scholarship focuses on a variety of issues in the sociology of religion, and focuses on liturgical worship and the new evangelization movement in Catholicism. He is currently involved with his collaborators, David Maines and Ben Bennett-Carpenter, in the study of how the New Evangelization is being implemented in parishes of the Archdiocese of Detroit. His wife, Catherine, and he reside in Clinton Township, Michigan and have three sons, ages 24, 21, and 13.

David R. Maines is Professor of Sociology and former chair of the Department of Sociology and Anthropology at Oakland University, Rochester, Michigan. He has held previous positions at Wayne State University, Penn State University, Northwestern, and Yale. His scholarly work has focused on developing a macro symbolic interactionist perspective, and he has published many papers on issues such as temporality, narrative, race, and other matters. His most recent work has been with his collaborator, Michael McCallion, on the Archdiocese of Detroit. His previous books include *The Faultline of Consciousness: A View of Interactionism in Sociology* (Aldine de Gruyter, 2001), *Social Organization and Social Processes: Essays in Honor of Anselm Strauss* (Aldine de Gruyter, 1991) and, with Carl Couch, *Communication and Social Structure* (Charles C. Thomas,

1988). He is the recipient of the George Herbert Mead Award for lifetime con-
tributions to interactionist scholarship, awarded by the Society for the Study of
Symbolic Interaction, as well as Oakland University's Research Excellence
Award.